International Socialism 101

International Socialism 101
Quarterly journal of the Socialist Workers Party (Britain)

Editor: John Rees. Assistant editors: Alex Callinicos, Chris Harman, John Molyneux, Lindsey German, Colin Sparks, Mike Gonzalez, Peter Morgan, Mike Haynes, Judy Cox, Jim Wolfreys, Sally Campbell, Megan Trudell, Mark O'Brien, Michael Lavalette, Sam Ashman, Rob Hoveman, Andrew Stone, Mark Thomas and Jane Hardy.

Published December 2003
Copyright © International Socialism
Distribution/subscriptions:
International Socialism, PO Box 82, London E3 3LH
Phone: 020 7538 3308
E-mail: isj@swp.org.uk
American distribution: B de Boer, 113 East Center Street, Nutley, New Jersey 07110

ISBN 1 898876 49 5

Printed by BPC Wheatons Ltd, Exeter, England
Typeset by East End Offset, London E3
Cover by Noel Douglas (info@noeldouglas.net)

A full index for International Socialism is available at www.lpi.org.uk
For details of back copies see the end pages of this book

Subscription rates for one year (four issues) are:
Britain and overseas (surface):
individual   £18
institutional   £25
Air speeded supplement:
North America   £2
Europe/South America   £2
elsewhere   £4

We welcome proposals for articles and reviews for *International Socialism*. If you have a suggestion, please phone or e-mail as above. All contributions should be typed and double spaced. The deadline for articles intended for issue 103 is 3 March 2004.

Contents

Editorial

Women have gained a fantastic amount over the last 30 years—a level of financial independence through work, and greater sexual freedom through contraception. But the positive changes have brought their own problems—women are now expected to be career women *and* house-proud mothers, with the cost of childcare beyond the reach of most workers. At a time when lapdancing clubs seem to be springing up faster than nursery schools, Lindsey German, author of *Sex, Class and Socialism*, looks at the reality of women's oppression today. She argues that the involvement of women in the growing global movement raises the possibility of bringing the fight for equality back to the centre of struggle.

In a world where millions of people are living on the brink of starvation while millions of others face obesity-related health problems due to fast-food diets, the politics of food is a vital question. Carlo Morelli takes a detailed look at some of the key players in the industry: Nestlé, Unilever and Sainsbury's. If, as he argues, the logic of the Project for a New American Century applies here, what are the implications for the struggle to regain control over our world?

Democracy is at the heart of the debates in the movement. In an extended review of Geoff Eley's *Forging Democracy*, Colin Barker charts the progressive movements which have shaped our world over the last 150 years. How has the left tackled 'the woman question', forms of organisation, and imperialist reaction?

Book reviews include Rob Hoveman on *After Theory* by Marxist cultural critic Terry Eagleton, and Phil Marfleet on Nigel Harris's paean to the market, *The Return of Cosmopolitan Capital*. Plus, Neil Faulkner replies to a critical review of his *Apocalypse: the Great Jewish Revolt Against Rome, AD 66-73*, published in *International Socialism* 98.

Women's liberation today

Lindsey German

Women are more visible than they have ever been in history. They perform much of the paid labour of the world and the majority of the unpaid labour. Women work the majority of total hours in the world, but work much less than men do for pay—and when they are paid they receive less wages.[1] Women's role in working outside the home raises their profile in all sorts of ways: they work in factories, in offices, driving buses and taxis. They socialise outside their home and family. They travel on public transport. They join unions and go on strike. And where there is protest there are likely to be women. In Britain the number of young women taking part strikes everyone who has been on the huge anti-war and anti-capitalist demonstrations. Women wearing the Muslim hijab mingle with those in miniskirts and fcuk tops. Picket lines of nursery nurses and council workers, but also of firefighters and post office workers, have strong representations of women. British Airways workers at Heathrow who went on strike showed that workers can wear uniforms and make-up and still be militant. School students who struck against the war in Iraq were usually led by women who showed themselves to be the most articulate and intelligent of the new generation. The new movements that we are witnessing are also movements of women. They stand in strong contrast to many of the older women who purport to represent them. The female cabinet ministers like Patricia Hewitt, the women executives and professionals who claim to represent the advance of feminism, have nothing to offer these women and are usually totally hostile to their aspirations and political views.

But women's public profile has not led to equality or an end to oppression. More freedom about sex has all too often meant exploitation rather than liberation. The obsession with the body which dominates society leads to women starving themselves and then binging on food, or paying large sums of money to enlarge breasts, straighten noses and temporarily banish wrinkles. Lapdancing clubs and lad magazines have become the new symbols of male chauvinism. The awareness of rape fostered by the women's movement in the 1970s created at least some understanding that 'whatever we say, wherever we go, yes means yes and no means no'. Now we are again confronted with the view that women's behaviour means that they 'asked for it' in some appalling rape cases. While far more women report rape now than in the late 1970s, the rate of conviction has fallen from 32 percent to 10 percent.[2] Women are constantly told that they can't have it all, but they are expected to do it all: be successful career women, devoted mothers, gourmet cooks, intelligent conversationalists and fantastic lovers. Financial independence remains an illusion when women earn at least a fifth less than men for the same jobs. Political equality is distant: women were very much at the heart of leading the anti-war movement in Britain, but in many campaigns men are over-represented. Platforms at events such as the European Social Forum are still heavily dominated by older white men. And while society may look equal in some areas, the closer you get to the powerful capitalist institutions like parliament or the City of London, the more male dominated they are.

Women in Britain are no longer expected to be sexually docile. They are encouraged by advertising and by a series of glamorous and high-profile images of women to make their sex lives exotic and adventurous. They are expected to have children at some point in their lives, but are not usually frowned upon if they do not. They are more likely than not to experience sexual relations before marriage, and are also likely to divorce. They marry later and have fewer children than their grandparents or great-grandparents. Girls are encouraged to prepare themselves for a career on the same basis as boys. But they carry their oppression into these changed sexual and social relations. Men are still on top metaphorically if not physically. Greater sexual freedom is a huge step forward for many women but it is still very far from genuine freedom and equality.

We have reached a stage in women's social development which would have been unthinkable only 50 years ago. Yet liberation is as far away as ever in the sense that it was developed as a theory and a strategy more than 30 years ago. That early movement was not mainly or even at all concerned with establishing more women managers or even female MPs. Instead it aimed to bring a greater sexual equality linked with what was widely recognised as the necessity of social change which could allow the development of women's liberation.

The women's movement began in the US and grew out of the great movements for social justice which dominated the 1960s there. Women had been involved in the civil rights movement, in the movement against the Vietnam War, in the 'new left' and in the student movement. They could not help but analyse their own oppression in similar terms to these other movements. The 'women's liberation workshop' which met in June 1967 articulated women's position as 'a colonial relationship to men', drawing an analogy with the Vietnamese or blacks in Africa, and concluding that therefore they had to fight for their independence: 'Only the independent woman can be truly effective in the larger revolutionary struggle'.[3] The women's movement was seen as part of bringing wider social change.

This was even more true in Britain. Who now remembers that women's liberation in Britain was very closely linked to the working class movement and to strikes? The dispute of Ford women workers for equal pay and that of the London night cleaners became well known, and celebrated as signs of women taking action to achieve equality. There were many other strikes at the time involving women: the teachers in 1969, the post office telephonists in 1971, and the Leeds clothing workers in 1970. It was the time of a growing and militant working class movement, and although the really big battles of that movement mainly involved men such as the miners and dockers, women's newfound militancy could not be ignored.[4]

The women's movement in Britain, unlike its much larger counterpart in the US, was influenced by this level of class struggle and by the working class movement. The input of socialists and trade unionists was much more apparent and more dominant in the movement as a whole than in the US. The movement also had as its backdrop the substantial legislative changes of the late 1960s and early 1970s: the legalisation of abortion, the easing of divorce, the decriminalisation of gay sex between consenting adults, and the laws introduced to implement equal pay and an end to sex discrimination.

Why has the early promise of liberation not been fulfilled, as many expected it would be? Women's entry into the workforce and their achievement of greater sexual freedom were rightly seen as striking great blows against women's oppression. But within capitalism the conditions under which these changes were achieved and the wider society in which they have developed tell us everything about why they fell far short of liberation. There has been a huge change in women's work worldwide: in countries such as China, Thailand and Indonesia rapid industrialisation has turned women into workers in factories and sweatshops in a modern parallel of the industrial revolution which transformed Britain 200 years ago. But many women from the poorer countries have to travel much further than from the country to the city. As well as making up a high proportion of the working class in their native countries, they all too often have to travel across the world in order to make a living. Migrant labour, much of it female, has brought women to work cleaning the houses of, caring for the children of or servicing sexually the Western middle classes. In the richest countries, women have been pulled into clerical work and retail work on an unprecedented scale, reflecting the growth of service industries in these countries over the past half-century.[5] All of these situations may have led to higher incomes or more independence (although this is by no means always the case) but they have all too often increased pressures on women, making their lives in some ways closer to men's, with all the stresses that entails.

A woman's work

Women's work has changed forever in the past 30 years and there seems to be no turning back. Women can no longer be seen as a peripheral part of the workforce. During the 1970s and early 1980s it was commonly claimed that women had been brought into the workforce in a time of boom and that when recession hit these workers would be the first to be made redundant. Women, it was said, were disposable workers in a way that men were not, and would be pushed back into the home. Their role in domestic labour and the part time nature of women's work would ensure that they were used as a reserve army of labour, content to stay outside the labour market in times of recession. So Anna Coote and Beatrix Campbell could write in 1982 that 'the great post-war boom in female employment has been abruptly halted and thrown into reverse'. Women, they argued, 'still represent a "reserve army of labour", to be called up and disbanded again, according to the vagaries of the economic and political climate'. To Coote and Campbell, 'Men are designated "real" workers. Women are not. Not only is their "right" to work illusory, but their foothold in the labour market is far more tenuous than they have supposed'.[6]

While this analysis has proved to be wrong, women have become a workforce characterised by low pay. And the working conditions of men and women, part time and full time, have noticeably worsened during the 1990s. The labour market has proved to be sex blind in the sense that women continued to be drawn into the workforce at an increasing rate while the bulk of job losses fell in areas which were heavily male dominated. The reasons for this were twofold: the structural changes in British employment led to a decline in manufacturing employment and a growth in various forms of service industry. Because of the occupational segregation of work in Britain, new jobs were increasingly likely to go to women. The second reason, however, was that the employers saw women as a pliant and flexible workforce.

By the beginning of the 21st century 70 percent of British women were in paid jobs, the largest proportion ever. This amounted to 12.5 million, an increase of nearly a million on ten years previously.[7] This increase in women working has only been made possible by more and more mothers going back to paid work rather than staying at home to look after their children. So a majority of women with children under five now work outside the home, and 65 percent of all women with dependent children do so. Nearly half of all single mothers are in work and almost a third of single mothers with children under five have some sort of paid work.[8] Of those women born in the first decade of the 20th century, only 30 percent who had children were working at the age of 30. Of those born between 1960 and 1963, 54 percent of those with children were. Sixty seven percent of all women aged 30 worked in 1993 (compared to 48 percent in 1963).[9]

While historically the biggest constraint on women continuing to work throughout their lives was motherhood, this is less and less the case. The maintenance of full time work patterns for large numbers of mothers is one of the biggest changes that has taken place: 'The number of women who work during pregnancy and return to work within nine to 11 months of the birth of their child has increased dramatically in recent years'.[10] Women with children are also working longer hours than previously, and the rate of increase for those with dependent children has grown faster than for those without children, with mothers of children under five increasing their average weekly work by four hours between 1984 and 1994.[11] There is no single reason why this change—which shows absolutely no sign of reversing—came about. The greater availability and acceptance by employers of maternity leave, women's desire or need for continuous employment especially in certain competitive work, and the desire to return for personal and social reasons are some. However, the main reason that mothers go out to work is economic. The importance of women's earnings to family income increased markedly in the post-war boom.[12] This increasing dependence on the female wage at least in part explains the increase in full time working for mothers.

Women in lower income groups have gone out to work to compensate for the low and sometimes falling wages of many working class men. Whereas before the 1980s the wives of higher-income men saw their employment increase most rapidly, from the 1980s onwards it was those wives of lower-income men who increased their employment fastest. The share of family income contributed by women grew fastest among families where men had low or median earnings. Without women's pay, the rate of poverty among married or cohabiting couples in the early 1990s would have been more than 50 percent higher than it actually was.[13]

The 1980s and 1990s marked an increase in the rate of exploitation for very large numbers of working people. Conditions worsened dramatically in some areas: people worked longer hours or were forced to accept split shifts which took up a great deal of what should have been leisure time in the working day. The introduction of greater 'flexibility' in the workplace led to the abolition of certain rights such as tea breaks. In some industries wages were actually cut—for example as a result of privatisation, where public sector jobs were reassigned at lower rates of pay, or in industries such as printing and journalism where the union-busting operations of Rupert Murdoch and Eddie Shah led to a general lowering of wages and worsening of conditions across the whole sector. Women were moving into work at precisely the time when unions were being weakened and established conditions and agreements were being torn up. The prospect of universal and affordable childcare, of decent conditions and of real improvements in women's lives appeared even more remote than it had done one or two decades previously. Now women were being told that they had to work, that childcare while they worked was their responsibility, and that it was also their responsibility to equip themselves to enter the labour market. On top of that they still had their family responsibility. The term 'double burden' doesn't begin to describe this situation.

Childcare

If the health service was run on the same basis as childcare in Britain, people would be lying bleeding to death in the streets and the vast majority of patients would have to rely on relatives or paid volunteers who already had to care for other sick people. Yet we expect millions of children of working mothers to be cared for by grandparents and other relatives, friends and other unpaid carers. The bulk of paid childcare is performed by registered childminders, often themselves mothers who cannot work outside the home. Only a small minority are cared for in nurseries or other childcare institutions. The post-war retreat on nursery provision and the ease with which part time work could be fitted in with childcare meant that publicly funded childcare provision never accompanied the post-war boom. Since the mid-1970s the consistent attempts to cut back on public spending have also meant that any universal and publicly provided childcare system has been denied to the millions of working women who could benefit from it. A major reason for mothers not working is lack of afford- able childcare. One study showed that a third of women who did not return to work after having a baby said they could not earn enough to pay for childcare. Of mothers who did not work, nearly a quarter said they would work full time with the childcare of their choice and a further 55 percent said they would work part time. Only 19 percent of non-working mothers said they would not work even with the childcare of their choice.[14] The gap between supply and demand has been calculated by the Daycare Trust as one registered childcare place for every 7.5 children under eight years old in England.[15] Although the vast majority of three and four year olds now have some form of nursery education, this is mostly not full time. The market rules in childcare, with miserly levels of full time state provision and with the onus placed on parents to find the resources—both family and financial—to pay for it. Childcare costs in Britain are the highest in Europe. At mid-1990s levels it was estimated that the cost of childcare for two chil- dren, one pre-school and one older, was £6,000 a year. It is estimated that parents meet 93 percent of childcare costs. Single parents who worked in the early 1990s were spending nearly a quarter of their earnings on child- care.[16] A typical nursery place now costs £6,200 a year.[17]

Promises by the Labour government to dramatically increase the amount and quality of childcare have not materialised. The shortfall in child- care is worse than in any other EU country, and the expense of what provision is available puts a heavy burden on working mothers, with some spending a quarter of their wages on care. There are just eight day nursery places for every 100 children under five. In the case of 62 percent of pre-school children and 77 percent of school-age children, parents use informal childcare by neighbours, friends and relatives.[18] After-school clubs are available for only one in 14 of school-age children.[19] The solution to this problem was that 'grandmothers would be paid for looking after their grandchildren under plans being drawn up by ministers to get more single parents back to work', according to the *Financial Times*.[20] One of the consequences of the failure of childcare has been the much lower level of workforce participation of single mothers compared with mothers in relationships. While, as we have seen above, mothers in couples have dramatically increased their work participation, this has not been the case for single mothers. A major reason for this is the lack of free or cheap childcare, making paid work barely worth doing for single women who cannot command an above-average salary. So 61 percent of single mothers do not work, and the problem barely changes when children first attend school, since mothers are still responsible for childcare before and after the school day and cannot work full time.[21] However, it is especially acute for mothers of under-fives, with less than a third of these single mothers in paid work.[22] Funding of childcare demonstrates the problems of scarcity, inefficiency and high cost: the vast majority comes from private individuals. Of total sector funding, £190 million comes from private companies, £50 million from miscellaneous sources, £150 million directly from the government and a gigantic £1,655 million from private individuals (of which £110 million is from government indirect subsidies).[23] So childcare becomes a tax on working men and women, which is often simply too onerous for them to afford.

Decent professional childcare over long hours is very expensive, making it a struggle even for many professionals. Live-in childcare is concentrated among the rich. 'The scarcity of nannies has driven up salaries and perks, making them the preserve of the very wealthy'.[24] A study that took place in 1990 drew the conclusion that 'practically all nannies or mothers' helps looked after children of professionals, employers and managers'.[25] The director of a charity, earning with her partner more than the £58,000 a year which would allow them tax credits, was quoted in the *Financial Times* as paying her nanny £250 a week to look after her two children full time. It is estimated that parents living in London have to set aside £35,000 gross income to pay for a professional nanny—as much as or more than the combined income of most working couples.[26] Nannies tend to care for pre-school children for the longest hours in any particular day, followed by registered childminders. Nannies are more likely to start early, finish late, and work five days a week. 'Informal' (or unpaid) childcare with neighbours or friends is much more likely to be for shorter hours during the day and for one or two days a week.[27] Income plays a large part in securing childcare and for many women this determines the work that they do: commuting and long hours are obviously much more difficult for women with young children unless they have sufficient income to pay for professional care over a long period of the day. Lack of childcare therefore often means relying on unpaid sources or limited paid provision, which in turn means working relatively near to home and often part time. For many working class families unpaid childcare is often the only option. The majority of pre-school children are looked after informally, mainly by fathers and grandmothers, when the mother is not there. When it comes to working mothers, the nature of childcare varies greatly according to class. The proportion using fathers and grandparents is much higher among manual workers than among professionals and managers. While 29 percent of professionals' and 27 percent of managers' children are cared for by fathers, 45 percent of children of skilled manual and 50 percent of children from semi-skilled manual families are cared for by them. Grandparents are the carers for 18 percent of children of professionals and 25 percent of children of managers and employers. This rises rapidly among intermediate and junior non-manual to 44 percent, the same proportion as the children of skilled manual workers.[28]

The family and the unskilled labour within it are still the scene of much childcare. The proportion of childcare paid for by the working class directly or provided free by their services in the home shows how successful the capitalist class has been in forcing working people to carry the costs of increased childcare involved in such a big expansion of the workforce. The burden this puts on individual families and the direct contribution it makes to continuing women's oppression are very great.

Poles apart

The class divisions within childcare reflect the wider class divisions within the female workforce. Many women now see their life as defined by their relationship to the labour market, but they don't all come to the labour market in the same way. It is commonly assumed that there is a polarisation in work between those in full time careers and those in casualised, low paid and part time work. This is one division but a more important one has taken place in women's work. A minority of women have risen up the ladder of success over the past two decades and now comprise the growing number of higher professionals, middle and higher managers, and business executives. They command salaries beyond the dreams of most working class women and men, and they find themselves in an increasing and often direct conflict with those they employ or supervise—often women. On the other hand, the mass of working women have found the pressure of work intensified as they enter the labour market in ever greater numbers. This pressure occurs in the supermarkets and call centres, but also in the more traditional 'female professions' such as nursing or teaching. Those in routine full time work are closer to those in part time and low paid work than they are to those in higher managerial or professional jobs. This is true in terms of wages and conditions as well as the fact that many women will move between the two in the course of their working lives.

This pattern was already under way nearly two decades ago. A perceptive commentary at the time talked of the double-edged nature of women's employment in 1988: 'Women's employment has been protected and expanded not because women are progressively overcoming their relative disadvantage in the labour market, but because of the continued existence of these disadvantages which causes them to be an attractive source of labour supply to employers for particular types of jobs.' Women were beginning to secure their position in the labour market 'by becoming more stable and continuous participants in the labour force and by actively increasing their levels of qualifications pre and post entry to the labour market'. But that would benefit only a minority, 'with the employment conditions for the majority deteriorating while an increasing minority acquire more of the characteristics...traditionally reserved for male labour'.[29]

A minority of women have gained substantial rewards in terms of income, status and the ability to pay for others to perform personal services such as childcare and cleaning. This minority have seen real advances as traditionally male areas have been opened up to women. Today a woman heads the London Stock Exchange and a third of all managers and administrators are women.[30] In 1997, 52 percent of new solicitors were women, 32 percent of managers and administrators, 34 percent of health professionals and 27 percent of buyers, brokers and sales reps.[31] This has been marked by a dramatic increase over two decades. Whereas in 1974 only 2 percent of directors and managers were women, by 2000 women made up 22 percent of this category.[32] However, these women have tended to accept the traditional ideology that they cannot take into account any of the aspects of being a woman that might put them at a disadvantage. A survey of executive women throughout Europe demonstrated that childcare benefits were their lowest priorities because 'they simply want to earn good money and make their own decisions about how to solve their childcare issues'.[33] Whatever their disadvantages in relation to men of their class, the relationship of these women to most working class women is managerial and often adversarial. The women in designer suits who drive expensive cars have become a part of working life—and most working class women are discovering that they get no special favours from women managers.

Then there are the other women in suits—this time the cheaper mass-produced ones from Next or BHS—or in uniforms. These are the mass of office workers, the uniformed bank and building society clerks, the nurses, the workers in Sainsbury's or Tesco. Add to them the teachers, childcare and welfare workers, the very young and female workforce in the call centres, and you have much of the female working class today. There are over 400,000 workers in call centres, large numbers of them women. The fastest-growing occupations throughout the 1990s tended to contain disproportionately high numbers of women: sales assistants and receptionists, education and health service workers, care assistants, welfare workers and nursery nurses. The fastest-growing single occupation was hairdressing.

These women in the majority are low paid, they are often engaged in routine and repetitive work, and they are subject to many of the traditional controls over work which were once confined to manual workers. Computerisation means that managers know exactly what a worker is doing at any one time. The introduction of machinery into office work has transformed the nature of work, with photocopiers playing the role of printers and word processors monitoring work, and nearly all work being tied to a machine. In shops the checkouts measure speed of throughput and act as stocktakers, placing new orders as they mark what is being sold. Even work which was once considered part of the professions—such as nursing, lecturing or teaching—is now subject to much greater managerial control, with many of the disciplines of the traditional factory job.

There is no fundamental difference in job description and lack of control between these workers and those who work part time. As we have seen, increasing numbers of women work full time when they are able to do so, but there are real barriers towards them doing so all the time. Low pay, childcare and other caring responsibilities mean that for at least part of their working lives many women will work part time. The sociologist Catherine Hakim has argued that most women are not interested in careers and prefer to centre their lives round childcare and home responsibilities. Only a minority of women, she says, want to work full time in high-powered jobs.[34] This argument only serves to justify the status quo, with its existing gap between high paid women and those part-timers who are presumably happy in their low-wage, low-status jobs. But the connection between part time working and family responsibilities is overwhelming. While care in the home remains privatised, millions of women will continue to work part time regardless of their aspirations, because they have no alternative. The historic *Women and Employment* survey of 1980—the biggest survey of women and work— showed that women working part time were more likely to be in 'women only' jobs. Over half of women part time workers finished work by 4pm to pick up the kids from school.[35] Of those couples with children, women who worked part time were more likely to work evenings than those working full time. Nearly one in 20 women part-timers with children also worked nights, suggesting that mothers take part time work when fathers or other members of the family can care for the children.[36] Satisfaction with part time jobs is clearly relative: a 1990s study showed that women part timers were overqualified for their jobs. Over half of women part-timers said that given their qualifications and experience they could expect a better job. They were less likely than full-timers to say their current job was the one they liked best.[37] There have been increases in recent years in the number of part-timers who would prefer a full time job.[38] Much has been made of the satisfaction which part time women feel in their jobs, and undoubtedly many do. But as Martin and Roberts, authors of the survey, commented, 'In some ways it is not surprising that such a high proportion of part time workers were happy with their hours of work; unless they can find a job with suitable hours they are unlikely to be able to work at all'.[39]

Women's wages—despite over 30 years of equal pay legislation—still lag behind men's. In 1998 women earned on average £6.67 per hour, 75 percent of men's hourly average of £8.94.[40] The distribution of female earnings tells how far away from equal pay women in Britain still are, despite real improvements. For a significant minority of women it is possible to earn as much as or even more than men. A fifth of women now earn more than their working partners, compared with one in 14 in the 1970s.[41] This testifies to the growth of a section of women able to earn as much as or more than at least some men. But it is not the main picture. Even by the mid-1990s, 20 percent of women earned less than or equal to the bottom 10 percent of men. Another more than 20 percent earned equal to the second lowest 10 percent of men. Only 3 percent of women earned equal to the top 10 percent of earners. Around three quarters of women fell into the bottom half of male pay distribution.[42]

Work has not held the key to liberation for women; rather it has meant exploitation on a similar basis to men, with the added burden of work in the home. While a minority have benefited from the conditions of the past two decades, the large majority of women are concentrated in some of the poorest jobs and in the worst conditions. The level of inequality is growing wider, and this includes inequality among women themselves.

The great leap forward

The impact on personal lives of the change in women's work patterns has been dramatic. Only half a century ago marriage was regarded as the only path to respectability for a woman. A child born outside marriage was viewed as a terrible and shameful burden in many families. Monogamy in relationships was promoted in women's magazines, by church, state and government. Geoffrey Gorer, author of a study in the early 1950s, regarded English sexual attitudes as remarkable. He wrote, 'I very much doubt whether the study of any other urban population would produce comparable figures of chastity and fidelity'.[43] Yet in 1997 there were 310,000 marriages, one of the lowest figures in the 20th century, of which only 181,000 were first marriages—a decline of more than half since 1970.[44] The proportion of women aged 18 to 49 cohabiting has more than doubled in the past two decades from 11 percent to 29 percent.[45] Divorce rates in Britain are twice as high as in any other EU country.[46] Teenage pregnancies are the highest in Europe—twice as high as Germany, three times as high as France and six times those of the Netherlands.[47]

What happened to bring about this change? There were two major advances in women's sexual behaviour during the 20th century. One was during the Second World War, where industrial and military conscription gave women sexual opportunities not previously available to them, and the dangers of war lent a greater urgency to relationships. But while this change had dramatic effects on divorce rates and numbers of children born outside marriage, the dominant post-war morality stressed domesticity and home-centredness. That this ideology was in increasing contrast with reality became fully apparent in the 1960s, which marked the real leap forward in terms of attitudes to sexuality and relationships. But this time the change was permanent and only deepened over time.

The movements and attitudes of the 1960s—at the heart of which is the sexual revolution—were a rebellion of young against old, in a society where the old had dominated the young for generations. Now all the attitudes were subverted—the work ethic, the patriotism, the deference and of course the sexual conservatism. The young were in a position where they did not have to just submit to the wishes of the old:

[In the early 1960s] there were a million more unmarried people in the age range 15 to 24 than ten years previously—a 20 percent increase. And they wielded a new economic power. Average real wages increased by 25 percent between 1938 and 1958, but those of adolescents by twice this. And though they disposed of only some 5 percent of total consumer spending, they were the biggest purchasers of certain commodities—42 percent of record players, 29 percent of cosmetics and toiletries, 28 percent of cinema admissions.[48]

At the same time, they tended to be dependent on their parents longer, through the raising of the school leaving age and the broadening of higher education. This led to greater tensions between parents and their children. So too did the more open attitude to sex, denounced as 'permissiveness' by much of society and the subject of continued controversy and debate. For most young people there were still many restrictions on sex. However, sexual intercourse was taking place at a younger age. So whereas for women born between 1931 and 1935 the median age of first intercourse was 21, for those born between 1941 and 1945 the median had fallen to 19 years.[49] But sexual experience for many does not appear to have changed too much. As a survey done in the mid-1960s showed, for most people early sexual experience was often conducted by trial and error. Sex 'just happened': when penetrative sex occurred for the first time it was unpremeditated for four fifths of girls and boys. By age 15, only one in 50 girls and one in 20 boys had had intercourse. First intercourse was not pleasurable for half of boys and two thirds of girls.[50] But the fact was that many taboos in behaviour had been lifted by the 1960s. Marriage tended to be at a younger age and by 1972 one in three of those marrying who had not previously been married were teenagers. Figures from 1969-1970 showed that one third of teenage brides were pregnant and 43 percent of all premaritally conceived births were to teenagers. In addition only 54 percent of births conceived premaritally were legitimised by marriage in the period 1964-1970. Illegitimate births were at 5.8 percent in 1961 (following 5 percent in 1951)—by 1976 the rate was 9 percent.[51] This does not necessarily suggest a greater awareness of sexuality or of control over women's own bodies, but it does suggest a much greater willingness to reject 'old-fashioned morals'.

There were three major changes in women's lives which began to have an influence on their attitudes. First a small minority gained access to higher education. There they encountered on the one hand liberal attitudes on a whole range of issues which encouraged them to think differently about their role as women. Did they have to see their future as marriage and motherhood or were there alternatives at least for educated and independent women? On the other hand, they were subject to petty restrictions on their lifestyles and sex lives which created great frustration and anger. Women undergraduates who were caught with a man in their room could be expelled from the college. In France the restrictions on men visiting women's rooms were one of the issues which led directly to the great student explosion of May 1968.[52] The second issue was the greater control by women over their own bodies which for the first time in history made it possible to separate out procreation from sexual enjoyment. The third major change was women's greater financial and social independence.

The 1960s also produced the great social movements for change which marked the first major challenge to the post-war consensus in the West. Out of these movements came those for women's liberation and gay liberation and these helped to ensure that the questioning of the old order brought with it a new sexual radicalism. The more open moral climate of the 1970s met with a backlash. The second half of the 1970s saw successive attempts to restrict abortion. James Callaghan's Labour government stressed the need for a strong family and for a return to more conventional education. The AIDS epidemic which began in the early 1980s was used as a means of attacking gay sex in particular.

There was a growing clash between the attitudes expressed by authority in society and people's real circumstances, their jobs and how they lived their lives. People had experienced open sexual relationships and they were determined not to give them up. So by the 1990s bigoted measures such as Section 28 of the Local Government Act, which banned the 'promoting of homosexuality' in schools, could continue to coexist alongside the creation of much larger and more open gay communities, at least in big cities such as London and Manchester. Government ministers could spout the virtues of the family while marriages fell to record lows and more people than ever lived outside the traditional family.

Sex and sexuality had been separated from procreation, so people quite rightly asked, why can't we gain sexual enjoyment in the way that we want—and what does it have to do with anyone apart from the individuals concerned? Whereas for previous generations there were all sorts of material constraints on sexual experimentation, by the 1980s and 1990s there were far fewer. Young people had more time, money and independence than their grandparents or parents. Particularly important in this were young women. Women have expressed an interest in sex which has shocked many people, but which is surely the natural outcome of a young generation with the usual interest in sex, but with the ability to do something about it. Women's assertiveness in this situation is a demand for the right to be treated equally with men, sexually as well as legally or financially.

By the beginning of the 21st century there were clear enough signs to point to certain permanent trends in love, marriage and sexuality. It was no longer the norm for people to abstain from sex before marriage—those who 'saved themselves' for marriage became a smaller and smaller minority.[53] Marriage itself had changed dramatically Whereas for some of the 19th century and much of the 20th premarital sex was taboo, now the norm was a form of 'trial marriage' with few social sanctions on either side if they broke the relationship—especially if children were not yet involved. Whereas in the 1950s only 1 percent of women in Britain marrying for the first time lived with the man for an extended period, by the early 1980s this rose to 21 percent.[54] Of those born between 1933 and 1942 in the US, 84.5 percent of men and 93.8 percent of women said they married without living with their partner beforehand; of those born between 1963 and 1974—only 30 years later—these figures had slumped to 33 percent of men and 35.3 percent of women.[55] As John Gillis has pointed out, 'The new cohabitation has many of the features of the old betrothal. It was an extended rite of transition—a liminal period—which was brought to a ritual conclusion when the couple decided it was time to incorporate themselves into the adult world of mothers and fathers'.[56]

Talk about sex and sexuality also tends to be more open, and sexual practices are more widespread and varied. There are marked differences between the generations. Only 3 percent of women who started having sex in the 1950s had ten or more lifetime partners, while 10 percent of women starting intercourse in the 1970s claimed this figure.[57] While half a sample of 45 to 59 year olds in the early 1990s cited 'being in love' as a reason for first intercourse, this reason declined through the age groups, to only 37.5 percent of women aged 16 to 24.[58] Attitudes to oral sex point to the changes which have taken place. A survey in the early 1990s revealed that while 76.7 percent of 18 to 24 year olds had experienced oral sex, this rose to 87.8 percent of 25 to 34 year olds but fell to 61.8 percent of 45 to 59 year olds. In the age group 16 to 24, of those who had ever experienced vaginal intercourse, 85 percent had also experienced oral sex. In the US oral sex appears to be increasing among virgins, with 25 percent of virgin boys and 15 percent of virgin girls having given or received oro-genital stimulation.[59] It seems the vast majority of oral sexual acts are reciprocal, rather than the blowjobs usually talked about in Hollywood films.[60]

Those who want women's equality can only welcome these developments, but the manifestations of sexuality which are so prevalent today cannot be said to add up to sexual liberation. Unlike the women's magazines of the 1950s, where sexual problems were referred to cryptically on the problem page, those of today trumpet advice on keeping your man happy, how to improve your sex life and so on. The assumption is that most people are having an active sex life most of the time, although this is very far from the case.[61] We are sold particular images of sex and sexuality which conform to certain stereotypes about men and women but which reinforce attitudes which are unequal or reinforce oppressive relationships: images of violence, of dominance and submission, of rape. The image of sex is far from one of equality and openness. Sex in all of its manifestations is seen as a commodity to be bought and sold on the market. Pornographic films, videos, magazines, lap-dancing clubs, phone sex, lad magazines with semi-pornographic contents, male strippers, entertainment for stag and hen nights, 'cybersex', sex contact listings in magazines, expensive women's underwear, sex toys and upmarket ice cream are only some of the goods which have made millions for mostly big business in the past 20 years. Their profits have been made out of the greater sexual openness: 'In 1996 Americans spent more than $8 billion on hard core videos, peep shows, live sex acts, adult cable programming, sexual vices, computer porn and sex magazines—an amount much larger than Hollywood's domestic box office receipts and larger than all the revenues generated by rock and country music recordings'.[62]

Globalisation helps create and characterises the sex trade. Sex tourism is a major part of the economy in a number of countries. In Thailand 'international tourist arrivals jumped from 2 million in 1981 to 4 million in 1988 to over 7 million in 1996. Two thirds of tourists were unaccompanied men... In 1997 the annual illegal income generated by sex workers in Thailand was roughly $10 billion'.[63] Estimates of the number of prostitutes in Thailand vary from more than 80,000, which is the government figure, to 200,000 or even 1 or 2 million.[64] In the Dominican Republic, popular with European male 'sex tourists', of 50 women working as prostitutes who were interviewed in a survey, all but two were single mothers pushed into the work through poverty.[65]

The destruction of the old industries and family structures worldwide has a major impact on these developments. Global inequality means that Western men can buy prostitutes very cheaply and that the women have to sell their bodies in order to survive. Governments ignore their plight most of the time. Those who constantly encourage the development of the free market, and who moralise at those who do not accept these developments, conveniently ignore this consequence of the market.

Freedom of sexuality should be a fundamental right, that people can enjoy sexual relations regardless of economic or religious constraint. Yet the increase in sexual freedom over recent decades, which should be of benefit to the vast majority of men and women, has brought buying and selling, the rule of the commodity, into what should be the most personal and intimate relationships. The women and men directly involved in the production and display of these commodities are often degraded by this process, but so are the rest of us, since sexuality is turned into a series of objects and commercial relationships rather than being a natural expression of human relations.

Housewives' choice

Changing sex roles have led to talk of male crisis. Hollywood films such as *Falling Down* or *Disclosure* paint the picture of a world where the old masculine values no longer apply and where women take cruel advantage over men at work. Men lose jobs to women, are sexually harassed by women, feel discriminated against by women. This makes them neurotic and ill (supposedly once the preserve of women). In the US 'movies featuring muscular men such as Russell Crowe and Brad Pitt [are] giving males an inferiority complex'. As record numbers of male subscribers to gyms were noted, US psychotherapist Roberto Olivardia commented, 'Men tie their self esteem to their physical appearance, it's a huge problem'.[66] Men now are much closer to women in their attitudes to physical appearance: they are more likely to follow fashion, to buy personal toiletries and to worry about their figure and looks. They are, however, more likely to become seriously ill than women, on average die younger than women and have a higher rate of suicide. In the ten years running up to the early 1990s, male suicides in Britain increased by 80 percent, notably among young men.[67] Nothing seems to be going right for men: increasingly they seem threatened by 'career women', frightened by their own failings as men and with a terrible sense of loss for the past golden age when men and women both knew their place.

Now men supposedly feel that they are superfluous to women and the family and no longer have a breadwinner role. The question could not even have arisen 30 or 40 years ago. Its starting point is the very great changes to the family and women's ability or desire to head a household. Whereas only 7 percent of households with dependent children were headed by lone mothers in 1971, by the late 1990s this had risen to 22 percent. Lone fathers headed another 2 percent of families.[68] These figures demonstrate a dramatic increase in the number of women caring for children without the support of a man. However, they also show that three quarters of children are still brought up in two-parent families. In addition, the sense that men have little or no role within the home hardly matches with their increased participation in childcare and housework. Most fathers who do not live with their children are not the 'deadbeat dads' of tabloid mythology. The majority are in contact with them: 70 percent of non-resident fathers have some contact with their children and 50 percent see their children every week.[69] So most children are living with or in regular contact with their fathers—hardly the basis for a mass crisis.

One feature of the change in men's behaviour has been the increase in male work around the home. This is a strongly contested issue: different surveys show different results, and surveys of who does housework are notoriously subjective. But there is general agreement that as women have ceased to be full time housewives, they have lessened the amount of work that they do in the home. As women work full time, so the gap between the amount of housework that they do and that of their male partners narrows. The number of hours devoted by men to household chores stood at 17 minutes per day in 1961; by 1985 it stood at 40 minutes a day.[70] During the same period the time spent by British women on routine housework fell by 55 minutes a day or 6.5 hours per week. In the initial part of this period the amount of housework done by men also fell, suggesting that the domestic appliances made affordable by the long boom were having some impact on curtailing hours spent in domestic labour. But that changed from the 1970s, when the domestic work of all men went up from 15 minutes to 40 minutes a day and that of full time employed from 13 minutes a day to 35 minutes. This 'probably therefore reflects ideological changes as well as the practical pressures associated with married women's move into paid employment'.[71] While the total number of hours spent on housework has fallen for all women it has not done so proportionately, with full time workers gaining least and with those without employment benefiting most.[72]

On the other hand, working parents of both sexes spend more time devoted to childcare—especially to under-five childcare. Employed men spent an average 44 minutes a day mainly on childcare in 1985 compared with 11 minutes in 1961—far less than the 107 minutes spent on the same childcare by women in 1985, but a substantial increase nonetheless.[73] Many men tell researchers that they would like to play more of a role in their children's lives than their own fathers did during their childhood.[74] However, the sexual division of labour is still one which sees women doing the bulk of domestic labour, despite the very great changes over the past few decades. A study in the mid-1990s for a Time Use survey showed that mothers spent much more time doing cooking and housework than men (2.59 hours per day as opposed to 0.41 hours) and more time caring for children and adults (1.56 hours against 0.54). Men on the other hand did more paid work (5.31 hours per day compared with 2.06 hours for women) and spent an hour a day on travel, compared with half an hour for women.

Women did, however, spend more time sleeping and socialising.[75] Recent statistics from the US give two examples of how family life is changing. Parents of both sexes are spending an average of ten or 12 hours less per week with their children than they did in 1960, and McDonald's is the source of 10 percent of family meals.[76] This suggests a family where everyone is under pressure of time and where the classic model of the family has been at the very least severely weakened in many respects.

The amount of work outside the home by either or both partners has a decisive effect on the amount of domestic work carried out by parents. The responses of young mothers and fathers, again in the mid-1990s, to questions about the division of labour in the home bear this out. Even when both partners worked full time, mothers took responsibility for the majority of household chores, but here 27 percent of men said they shared preparing and cooking the meal, 40 percent shared shopping and 35 percent shared cleaning equally. When the woman worked part time this fell to 15 percent, 28 percent and 16 percent. Where the wife was at home full time, only 10 percent shared cooking the main meal and only 11 percent shared cleaning—interestingly, the same number shared shopping as those with part time worker wives. Mothers' responses to the same questions showed some differences but not massive discrepancies. In general, women were slightly more likely to answer that they did most of these chores and slightly less likely to believe they were shared equally.[77] The overwhelming conclusion is that where both work full time they are most likely to share chores, but even then they are far from being equally shared. The traditional division of labour still applies, and men do most DIY and repairs. Even so, where the wife works and the man stays at home, the man's share increases, although not sufficiently to reverse roles. This is also the area of greatest discrepancy between men and women, so 28 percent of men believe they do most cooking of the main meal, while only 6 percent of wives think their husbands do this.[78] Some commentators have even suggested that men in full time work actually do more domestic chores than unemployed men with working partners.[79] It appears that that there are much more complex issues at work than simply who works longer hours outside the home. Where the sex roles are most obviously reversed—where the woman works and the man stays at home—there are often signs that the man has particular difficulty fitting into the 'housewife' role, while the woman both works outside the home and has to shoulder a substantial domestic burden as well. If this is the case, it suggests an ideological as well as a practical reluctance by some men in the home to take on this role, itself a product of the low esteem in which housework is held, which in turn comes from the nature of housework as repetitive and unpaid work inside capitalist society.

In a capitalist society the ability to sell one's labour power is the defining feature of each individual. Today the desire of capital for this labour power is so great that every member of the family is under pressure to enter the labour market. Anyone who is unable to enter this market finds himself or herself at a disadvantage. There are few opportunities for consumption of anything but the basic necessities of life. Those without paid work carry some of the lowest status in our society. Men who have been brought up to expect paid work as their right feel it particularly acutely when it is lost, and feel that being asked to fulfil a role which is widely seen as socially subordinate is a denial of their role as men. It is hardly surprising that those men who are forced from the labour market feel disoriented and without social value. This after all was how many housewives felt, and still do feel—but the men lack their social conditioning to be able to cope, hence their inability to even become 'good housewives'. Unemployed men who are responsible for childcare see themselves mostly as 'failed providers' rather than successful childcarers.[80]

Miners at Yorkshire's Grimethorpe colliery, which shut in 1993, describe the feelings of men in this situation. One says, 'My day? I get up and do the washing, hang it on the line, get the kids to school, do some shopping, get the tea for when she gets home... The government talks about training, education. What for?'[81] Another says, 'We had pride in our work, we made a contribution to the world, we had a place, a proper purpose. Gone. Now I'm a housewife'.[82]

One of the reasons many men's attitudes are so contradictory is because the signals sent to them by society are also contradictory. Much of the dominant ideology in countries like Britain is egalitarian in tone. Received opinion among the majority of our rulers and the bulk of the media is that men and women are both expected to work (indeed the stay at home mother who expects an income from the state is now regarded with disapproval). Men and women are expected to share housework and childcare where practically possible and families are deemed to operate as contented units of consumption where a degree of democratic choice is allowed to all its members. Men who behave as authoritarian father figures are regarded as both rare and wrong-headed. Tony Blair and David Beckham demonstrate that caring comes naturally to fathers. No one could call them Mary Annes—as they did men in Lancashire in the 1940s—when they push the pram[83] (not that they do it very often since that is the nanny's job). But even while men are being encouraged to show their emotions, there are much less pleasant developments which also have an ideological effect on men's attitudes to themselves. Traditional male values have also reasserted themselves, at least among a layer of men: lap-dancing clubs, new lad magazines, an insidious campaign against the notion of 'date rape', a resurgence of sexist language, and continuing high levels of violence against individual women.

The 'New Lads' with their old attitudes about women were a phenomenon described thus by Simon Nye, writer of the television series *Men Behaving Badly*:

> The Lad was created by the meritocracy (or new plutocracy, depending on your political allegiance) unleashed by Margaret Thatcher in 1979. The shouty young men that crowded London's trading markets and exchanges, earning fortunes and scaring away cupboardsful of sniffy Guildford stockbrokers, were the Trojan Lads, hidden in the bellies of financial institutions and wheeled inside the walls of the establishment. And it was okay to swear and be a bit of a sexist because they worked *bloody* hard.[84]

The main expression of the 'lads' has been the rise of the men's magazines—glossy and upmarket, filled with expensive advertising, by the late 1990s they were selling 1.5 million copies a month between them.[85] The titles range in sophistication and presentation but there is no doubting their selling point: the covers always have women in various states of undress. The inside is little different, containing vast amounts about sex, a lot of football, and a very strong interest in conspicuous consumption. There is a general assumption that 'foreigners' are inferior, being both strange and stupid, that women really 'want it' according to the most stereotyped male fantasy, and that any real man will only be interested in beer, sport and 'shagging'. But these are aspirational men behaving badly. The editor of *GQ Active* described his average reader as between 25 and 35 and likely to be 'cruising down the motorway in an Audi with a mountain bike on the roof'.[86] Advertising is aimed at twenty- and thirty-somethings with large amounts of disposable income, focusing on cars, clothes and army recruitment.

It is sometimes argued that the lad phenomenon and the men's magazines have a positive effect, that they are 'an attempt by straight men to come to terms with their new position in the world, with the second wave of feminism and the undermining of traditional forms of gender identity'.[87] But any inspection of these magazines shows little understanding of coming to terms with very much. Features in *Loaded* include 'Ten great arse moments in movies' or David Baddiel's views on wanking. In *FHM*, which is supposed to be more sophisticated, international analysis is at the boys' comic level. This is Benny Hill humour repackaged for the 1990s, and underlying it is a deeply conservative set of values. In this they resemble the 1950s too. Women who complain about such images, who don't find the sexist jokes funny, or who in any other way break from the norm, are regarded as humourless, too unattractive to get a man, or lesbians. We love women, is the cry of the new lads, but they don't love women at all. The love a particular stylised and objectified image of women because they believe this enhances their masculinity and status:

> In the case of lad mags there is not only nostalgia for images of women in the mode of *Playboy* at its heyday, but also the desire to utter all the offences known to man, freed from the imagined tut-tutting of 'ardent' feminists. Men's magazines celebrate images which three decades ago feminists would have denounced without hesitation; but these contemporary images are set in a context which attempts to deny us the right to have any opinion at all.[88]

The message of the magazines is that men can still celebrate their domination in the face of the threat of liberation—and who can dare to complain? Old sexist activities are dressed up as fun in other areas as well. Sleazy old stripping is reborn as lapdancing in expensive clubs patronised by businessmen and those on outings from City banks. The presence of women in the audience is supposed to make this cultural development acceptable. The 200 clubs which now exist in Britian mark 'the invention of a branch of the sex industry considered not the slightest bit exploitative, nor remotely damaging to women'.[89] The lapdancing clubs, however, do not break the mould of the old exploitative strip joints or brothels—rather they repackage it for credit card customers.

The alibi for much of this behaviour is the existence of women who participate: the ladettes—hard-drinking, sexually aggressive, confident women who are supposedly happy to go along with this because they are playing men at their own game. The old sexism wanted women to be passive—now they are allowed to be active as long as they accept sexism. This wanting to be one of the boys attitude goes much further than young women, with older women wanting to stress their continuing sexual attractiveness and activity. The middle-aged, middle class women who take their clothes off in *Calendar Girls*, Germaine Greer's writing on the boy as sex object and even the advert for Marks and Spencer's credit card where a woman eyes up the Italian waiter all show how lacking in subversion and reinforcing of sex roles this has become.

Part of the debate about men is about trying to shore up traditional family values in the face of an increasing unwillingness on the part of many people to live in the conventional nuclear family. Melanie Phillips declares that the 'so called "crisis of masculinity"' is 'invented by those who wish to claim that the distinctive role of fathers is redundant'.[90] Her aim is transparent—forcing men to work would solve many of the social problems that confront those who run our society at present:

> Male breadwinning…is neither arbitrary or anachronistic. It is important both to cement masculine identity and to civilise aggressive male characteristics. That's why unemployment has played havoc with young boys' socialisation and shattered their fathers' emotional and physical health. Employment is an instrumental, goal-driven activity which permits men to serve their families through competition. In that way it directs male aggression into pro-social purposes.[91]

The Phillips view of men is the modern equivalent of those who in the 1960s decried the absence of a war or national service into which young men could be conscripted. Today those who are excluded from work are accused of tending to turn to violence and—even worse—allowing the state to take responsibility for their families. Men have to know their place, and it is to work—the only means, in her chilling phrase, of 'civilising' them. If this authoritarian picture of an orderly world where men are breadwinners and women accept a traditional role as mothers and wives suggests that men have a built-in tendency to violence and bad behaviour as men, it is by no means unique. The sense that men can only be redeemed and civilised by the family is quite widely held.

Sandy Ruxton puts forward an explanation of the link between masculinity and criminality in the sex roles which men and women adopt when they become adults. The contradiction between the male child and the adult is greater than that between the female child and adult:

> The dominant view of masculinity is that a man should be tough, strong, aggressive, independent, rational, intelligent, and so on. But the dominant image of children is that they are vulnerable, weak, immature, passive and dependent. This creates a particular contradiction for boys, which is heightened as adulthood gets nearer, simply because, within the construction of childhood, being a man cannot be achieved.[92]

If this is true, then becoming a man means rejecting all the traits most closely associated with childhood—and which all too often are also associated with 'femininity'—and adopting behaviour and practices regarded as manly. Gangs, a degree of criminal behaviour, fighting, and scorning certain forms of learning which are seen as childish are all part of this process. So too is the adulation of sporting heroes. There is a class element to this. High-status schools tend to foster a liberalised version of the old public school ethos: individual excellence in sport, but also a sense of purpose in learning, given the expectation of all concerned in these enterprises that their pupils will fulfil an important place in society. The middle and upper classes place much store on individual development, to a certain extent apart from the mass of people, and an ambition to succeed in a career. Teenage boys from these sorts of backgrounds will see themselves as preparing for such a future. Working class boys take their adolescent development much more from the streets and from popular culture: collective praise for individual sporting or musical expertise is highly valued, and practical and physical attributes attract a higher status than academic ability. This is the sort of masculinity which is so objected to by the commentators, yet in itself it represents a threat not to the mass of people but to the dominant ideology which tries to put working class kids in their place. Why should ability at breakdancing not be valued as highly as playing golf? Or the ability to memorise song lyrics as valuable as knowing multiplication tables? The fashion for street clothes, the customisation of school uniforms, the refusal to accept the narrow middle class ideology now imposed with such a straitjacket on the schools, are a form of rebellion which often stresses aggression as a means of asserting some sort of control and status in life.

Even here we should hold on to some perspective. Most boys are not extremely violent, or habitual criminals. Some of the most common crimes may be more 'feminine' than 'masculine'. Home Office figures confirm that an eighth of all recorded offences are for shoplifting and that more women than men are cautioned for the crime. It is especially common among young women, and 7,528 girls between the age of 13 and 15 are cautioned each year. This compares with 6,370 boys.[93] One survey found that 89 percent of 16 year old working class girls had been involved in at least one physical fight.[94] It would be hard to deduce from recent furores around some of these questions that juvenile crime was not pandemic. Nor would one conclude that—as is the truth—more boys pass exams than in the past and there is less illiteracy among the young than among the old. It is true that in many areas of education girls do better than boys, and that their improvement rate tends to be much faster than boys. But this is hardly surprising given the transformation of expectations about work and education for women over the past few decades. Back in the 1950s and 1960s, when girls tended to do worse in education than boys, this was put down to girls' low expectations of a career and their internalisation of their oppression. Today, especially when educational qualifications have taken on such heightened importance in the labour market for workers of both sexes, it is hardly surprising that girls attempt to equip themselves for competition in that market alongside boys. It may be as well that the preponderance of girls in clerical and white collar jobs may encourage them slightly more than boys to gain qualifications. This is very much a process of equalisation between the sexes. In this process boys can feel that relatively they are doing worse and feel a lack of self esteem due to this. However, the fact remains that the position of boys in education is improving too, but at a much slower rate. The proportion of young women in Britain achieving two or more A-levels has doubled since the mid-1970s, whereas the number of men doing so has risen by just under a half in the same period. Even so, the number gaining A-levels has risen substantially.[95] Whereas 173,000 women were full time undergraduates in 1970/71, by 1997/98 there were 554,000. Comparable figures for men were 241,000 and 498,000. Women have caught up and overtaken men at this level, but among postgraduates they are still slightly below the figures for men, although again they have started from a lower level.[96] The big increase in women's participation and rise in qualifications seems to have stemmed from the 1980s, perhaps the most decisive decade in marking the idea that women had to take responsibility for their own self advancement, and this advance has certainly continued into the 1990s.[97] Whether it will continue—marking an ever widening gap between the sexes—or whether it will stabilise with broad levels of equality but with women at a slight advantage is too early to say. What is indisputable, however, is the role of class in education and this appears to have a much greater influence on performance than gender. Pupils in comprehensive schools in the poorest urban areas achieve half the success rate at GCSE of those in better-off urban areas.[98] In 1991/92, 55 percent from families of professionals went into higher education aged under 21; by 1998/99, 72 percent did. In 1991/92 only 6 percent of those from unskilled working class backgrounds went into higher education. By the end of the decade this had risen to 13 percent. Professionals were more than twice as likely as the national average to see their children in higher education, while unskilled workers were more than half as likely.[99] The sense of worthlessness and bitterness at what the future holds must surely be connected in the minds of working class girls and boys with this lack of accessibility to the sort of education which at least holds out a promise of financial and social benefits. For when we look at those children who gain no qualifications, there is not a massive discrepancy between boys and girls. So 8 percent of boys and 5 percent of girls gained no graded GCSEs in 1997/98, while 26 percent of boys and 33 percent of girls gained two or more A-levels.[100] Seeing the educational divide as a boy/girl question only obscures the much greater division of class which the right wing commentators are so keen to deny.

What sort of a society sees women as a threat?

Now men know what it's like to be a woman, is the common response from many of those women who find themselves regaled with stories of male crisis. Women can't help thinking that we've always had to put up with this—why is it different when it happens to a man? Time and again, the experience of men who have lost work or are doing lower grade work than they have been used to is comparable to women's traditional malaise at being in the home. Bill Costas, an unemployed meatpacker in the US aged 34 moans, 'I don't see anybody anymore. The guys I worked with were my buddies... We'd go out after work and have a beer and shoot the bull. Now I don't even know what they're doing anymore'.[101] Some believe men's problem is precisely that they are in the traditional 'female' role.

But of course they are not in the traditional female role. Men still go out to work in very large numbers, they still hang on to nearly all the really powerful jobs in capitalist society, and they still leave women holding the baby most of the time, whether these women do it for love or for a paid wage. Men are not full time househusbands very often—and those who claim to be are often working at home part time in an occupation which has a high degree of autonomy and is relatively well rewarded. This is a very long way from the low-status work, cut off from any society wider than immediate neighbours and children, that makes women prone to depression, boredom and nervous illness. Those men who most closely approximate to such a role are the long term unemployed, usually without direct childcare responsibilities, and often older men, who sense their worthlessness from their inability to sell their labour power.

The real transformation here is that men and women are moving closer together in terms of their work and their domestic life, but they are struggling to do so in conditions not of their own choosing. They do so against a background of continuing women's oppression and intensified exploitation for both men and women. No wonder so many feel in crisis. No wonder either that increasing numbers are beginning to question a society which treats men and women in this way. The experience of capitalist society is a potential unifier of working class people: the very process of exploitation brings large numbers of people together as workers. They face similar experiences of low wages, petty rules at work, the tyranny of time-keeping, and being constantly tied to machinery. They perceive a common enemy in the form of the employer. But there are other factors at work: most importantly, capitalist society also acts to divide working class people. This is done in a thousand small and large ways, and through a combination of ideological and material factors. Women's material disadvantage in terms of wages, for example, is underpinned by the view of women as primarily mothers or sex objects which still prevails. Racist and nationalist arguments feed on the fact that in capitalist society there is scarcity amid plenty and that workers have to compete for scarce resources. So competition between workers for jobs or housing or education can act to reinforce racist ideas. Society tries to pit men against women, blacks against whites, Catholics against Protestants. When an oppressed group gain anything at the expense of those they are supposed to be competing with, this is enough to cause a crisis. Instead of seeing the real source of problems lying in the wider social system which exploits and oppresses, working people all too often see the problem as lying within the immediate division of these scarce resources.

Women have not benefited at the expense of men. They still work in the home and in paid work. Both sexes are under increased pressure, with the lives of working men and women unrecognisable compared with one or two generations ago. Both now have to work to provide an adequate family income; both are pressurised to ensure that their children gain the education and qualifications to equip them for the labour market as it is today; both struggle to fit the tasks of childcare and housework into their busy lives. As the family becomes a centre of enhanced consumption, so individual men and women are sold an image of themselves which goes well beyond the old roles of breadwinner and homemaker. They are meant to successfully transcend these old roles and adopt at least some of the roles seen as the property of the other sex. Fitting into these new roles may be more rewarding or enjoyable in some cases, but it is usually hard work. So women work for less than equal wages while men are expected to participate in unpaid childcare.

The discomfort which men feel at the new situation in which they find themselves demonstrates how artificial the old situation was. In *The Condition of the Working Class in England* Frederick Engels wrote of the unease felt among men as they lost their work in textiles and saw their wives or daughters earning more money than they could. He described the plight of a male worker in St Helens, Lancashire, interrupted by a friend while darning his wife's stockings. The worker describes how he has had no work for three years, while his wife works from dawn till night in the factory and so is too tired to do anything at home.[102] Engels wrote of how insane this system was and how degrading it was to both sexes, since it 'unsexes the man and takes from the woman all womanliness without being able to bestow upon the man true womanliness or the woman true manliness'.[103] There is nothing natural about gender roles or about the attitudes and status which are attributed to them. Instead, he says:

> ...so total a reversal of the position of the sexes can have come to pass only because the sexes have been placed in a false position from the beginning. If the reign of the wife over the husband, as inevitably brought about by the factory system, is inhuman, the pristine rule of the husband over the wife must have been inhuman too.[104]

In an unequal society, there must always be someone on top—but there is nothing natural or fair about this. This is the basis of Engels' argument, developed elsewhere, that the family and gender roles within it are artificial constructions.[105] The male crisis is a product of a society incapable of treating its members as equal human beings, but which instead robs them of any control of their lives. The response to this among men in particular is twofold. Men often cling on to a sense of identity or pride in masculine values or traits, which they think set them apart from women (or indeed from men who are regarded as being 'feminine'). But at the same time they feel a sense of unease and of powerlessness in controlling what happens in their world. This explains much of the seemingly contradictory behaviour of men today and also points to a possibly frightening but potentially exhilarating future, as an understanding of the shallowness and inequity of the old relationships leads to a wider questioning of how the world is run.

The problem of feminism

What has happened to women's liberation? By the late 1970s the movement which had such an impact ideologically in putting the issue of women on the political agenda was deeply divided. The activism that marked many of its adherents declined dramatically; the women's movement had never been a mass movement in Britain, but now it fragmented into different and disparate campaigns. Although the movement's founders tended to be socialists and trade unionists, the second half of the 1970s saw the growth of radical feminism. The disputatious conference in 1978 marked the last time that the movement ever met as a movement. The subsequent decades have been ones of retreat for most feminists as the attempts to find niches where they could practise their feminism took them into different directions. Many saw the Labour Party and especially local Labour councils as a key agent of change, enthused by the chance of setting up women's committees and creating reforms for women as part of a reborn local government. The attacks by Thatcher on the GLC and other local councils put paid to such good intentions and little was salvaged from what remained apart from a number of individual women who went on to become MPs or councillors. Other women went into academia, teaching women's studies courses and related topics.[106] In the course of the 1980s and 1990s, as feminism became more acceptable as an ideology, so it became more limited in terms of what it would accept. Abandonment of collective change leads to an exclusive emphasis on individual change and with that powerlessness in confronting the structures of oppression. Instead of defining itself in solidarity with wider movements and with the working class struggle it was enough simply to think in a feminist way in order to be involved in political practice. This took its toll not just on the activism of the movement but on its ideas, especially as the right wing ideas of Thatcherism and then of neo-liberalism post-1989 gained influence. Some of the ideas which had been accepted in the 1960s and 1970s now came under attack: a generation of younger feminists sang the praises of make-up and designer clothes, or dismissed the idea of date rape as wildly exaggerated. In *The Morning After* Katie Roiphe writes, 'If I was really standing in the middle of an epidemic, a crisis, if 25 percent of my female friends were really being raped, wouldn't I know it?' Probably not, if in real life she is as unsympathetic to the problem as her book suggests, someone who believes that 'someone's rape may be another person's bad night'.[107] Another US feminist, Naomi Wolf, embraces the entrepreneurial spirit of the age with her attacks on 'victim feminism' and the belief that 'women's businesses can be the power cells of the 21st century'.[108] Wolf sees Princess Diana as someone to be admired for having transformed herself from being a victim.[109] British feminist Beatrix Campbell saw the pampered princess as the subject for a whole book, including the ludicrous claim that, 'By telling her story, Diana joined the "constituency of the rejected"—the survivors of harm and horror, from the Holocaust, from world wars and pogroms, from Vietnam and the civil wars of South America and South Africa, from torture and child abuse—who have transformed the work of storytelling in our century'.[110] Feminism appeared either disconnected from the world or desperately looking for role models to whom women could aspire—even if the role models turned out to be princesses.

Ideas of liberation do not stand in isolation from the wider society. Some of them can become incorporated or accepted within society— witness the very limited inclusion of a minority of women and an even smaller minority of blacks into the high echelons of power. Others adapt and bend to the dominant ideas, even where they are not totally abandoned. This happened to a layer of feminists who disconnected their individual progress from the wider progress of society. While working women in most parts of the world saw their conditions worsen, those who benefited from the changes left them behind or even blamed them for their own failure to change and to take advantage of the market opportunities which availed them. Identity politics projected a view which could only be about individual women 'getting on' and therefore encouraging other women. But the narrow scope of the vision led to myopia: identity politics could only see its proponents' own advances or otherwise. In a period when globalisation, imperialism and neo-liberalism have run riot, concern about individual women or blacks 'making it' has, as Naomi Klein so well puts it, 'amounted to a rearranging of the furniture while the house burnt down'.[111] Fighting over the shrinking resources available to women and blacks in the 1990s meant 'fighting their battles over a single, shrinking piece of pie—and consistently failing to ask what was happening to the rest of it'.[112]

Today there is barely any pretence from some erstwhile feminists that anything needs to be changed. A progression of spokeswomen for the successful minority now tell us that feminism is backward-looking or that women can only achieve by competing on the same terms as men.[113] The retreat even further into postfeminism has led to an abandonment of any attempt to make sense of women's oppression, but rather has become a simple reflection of one of society's dominant images—that women can make it if they work hard and don't cause any trouble. Elaine Showalter, veteran US feminist, now criticises the 'dead-end feminist combination of dependence on the nanny state and lack of enterprise in politics and popular culture' and urges us to 'solve the childcare problem, and also make money'. She asks, 'Where are the female Richard Bransons and Jamie Olivers of the nappy and naptime brigade?'[114] Where indeed?

The cleavage within the ideas of women's liberation runs along lines of class. Those who see liberation in terms of individual advance can only do so by ignoring the millions of women and men for whom life choices are quite different from which brand to buy, which car to drive, or how to achieve the best 'work-life balance'. Throughout the world, the conditions of these people have deteriorated while a small number have gained. Feminism has run up against the limits of class society: the existence of a small minority of women with access to top jobs and all the material advantages that these bring with them is perfectly compatible with the continued existence of class exploitation; millions of women achieving real change in the form of equal pay or socialised childcare is not. For the capitalist class to grant such demands would mean cutting deep into their profits, something they are unlikely to do without being forced to. And as the struggle revives, globally and in Britain, as it has over the past few years, questions of class become more relevant.

A growing number of women depend on other women to do their domestic labour. In the US between 14 and 18 percent of households employ an outsider to do their cleaning. Socialist feminist Barbara Ehrenreich says, 'Among my middle class, professional women friends and acquaintances, including some who made important contributions to the early feminist analysis of housework two and a half decades ago, the employment of a cleaning person is now nearly universal'.[115] But the question of class isn't simply about individual attitudes, shocking though some of these are—it is about the organisation of the whole of society.

The women's movement has failed because its theory was and is incapable of addressing the very big problems now facing women and the increasing class nature of the attacks on them. The theory of patriarchy, which locates women's oppression outside of capitalist social relations and tries to separate out oppression and class, proved inadequate to explain the real position of women. It could only explain women's oppression in terms of the benefits which accrued to men and to capital as a result of that oppression. Patriarchy could not therefore begin to explain the changes in women's lives which have been the themes of this article. Women went out to work because capital needed labour reserves during its long boom which could not be met by the existing male-dominated workforce. Women's entry into work coincided with large-scale immigration for the same reason. The wages of men and women needed to cover the higher costs of reproduction of the family, including the costs of childcare. The monogamous, lifelong marriage and the Kellogg's cornflake advert traditional family no longer fitted this situation. Sexual attitudes changed as a result of all these other changes, as women saw themselves as less and less subservient.

Capitalism has served to break down many of the oppressive structures which had dominated for hundreds if not thousands of years, but it could not create liberation because it acts to turn everything into a commodity and so even the caring functions of the family are increasingly bought and sold on the market. And it recreates oppression and its structures in order to divide the working class. The central arena of women's oppression remains the family, which is both broken down by the effects of capitalism and also maintained and reinforced by capital as the cheapest, most convenient and most socially stable way of caring for the existing generation of workers and reproducing the next generation.[116]

Liberation now?

What does liberation mean for a young woman in Thailand, facing the choice between hard factory work and prostitution under the control of pimps who exploit young girls for a few years until they lose their health or looks? What does liberation mean for a working mother in the north east of England who works in a call centre, who rarely sees her partner because they both work shifts, and who struggles to make ends meet on two miserable wages? What does liberation mean for the Hispanic cleaner in Los Angeles, threatened with deportation as an illegal immigrant and forced to neglect her own home to clean other people's?

It is obvious that political equality is not enough. Equality on the same basis as men is fine if the man you are comparing yourself to has an above-average income, can afford to pay for high quality personal services, and has more than adequate living space and a fulfilling high status job. If on the other hand he is low paid, works in a monotonous and highly supervised job, works unsocial hours and can only afford the cheapest housing, then the aspiration has to be for something more. The call then has to be for economic and social change, which means challenging the way capitalist society is organised. For many feminists this is not a necessity: positive discrimination at work, women-only shortlists for parliamentary elections, women managers and academics at the highest level, are sufficient to fulfil their aspirations. They do not even find these battles particularly easy, as we have seen from the pitifully small number of women MPs, or the regularly occurring industrial tribunals about sexual harassment of female high-fliers in the City of London. Institutions which defend privilege in general are unlikely to open up even to the most respectable or compliant women. But these feminists have little concern with these wider battles. Those who want to change the world for working class women have to look to more radical solutions.

The problem of childcare being privatised and remaining a burden for women cannot be solved unless we have at hand the resources of the whole of society to do so. That means the wealth that we create going not into the pockets of the already rich and powerful, but into developing a whole range of options for childcare including nurseries on every street or estate available free to all those who want to use them. A national childcare service based on the principles of the NHS would be a huge step forward, but no capitalist class in the world will let providing one eat into its profits when they can fall back on the family to do the work unpaid. The 35-hour week for men and women would be a huge step forward, cutting into unemployment, giving people much more leisure time and allowing them to spend more time with their children. This in turn would mean people needing less of the paid services which accompany the long hours we work: the cleaners, the grocery delivery vans, the childminders. Decent, cheap social housing would mean less travel and commuting to work as people were able to afford to live close to work. All of these provisions would benefit most women *and* men, as well as the wider society, but they will not be realised while those who control our world continue to do so, because they would cut into the profits of our rulers.

Liberation will only be achieved when the working people of the world take control of it, ending the exploitation which dominates our lives and destroys our human potential and relations. Revolution is about liberation and about taking control: control of the workplaces and the work process so that we produce for need, not profit; control of our own lives as we grapple with the possibilities of changing the world. For women that control is central because it also means sexual control in the genuine sense, rather than in the caricatured way of mimicking men it means today. Sexual control means the right to have children or not, as a woman chooses. This should seem a basic right in the 21st century, but there are women who are forced to have children they do not want because they are denied abortion or contraception. There are other women who are forced not to have children, injected with contraceptives such as Depo Provera. There should be no financial, political or moral pressure on these decisions. Women and men should have the right to divorce when either partner wants it. Women should be free from domestic violence and workplace sexual harassment. Only when we end an exploitative class society which maintains oppression at its centre can we take control and achieve these aims collectively.

The examples of even short-lived socialist societies in history demonstrate that women's demands came to the fore and that women themselves fought to achieve them. Post-1917 Russia, despite being poor, wartorn and beleaguered by invasion, achieved real changes for women in what had been one of the most oppressive societies in the world, changes only finally defeated with the rise of Stalinism. Women's liberation has to be part of the fight for socialism, of the overthrow of class society, for it to achieve any of its fundamental aims. If it is to be successful that struggle has to involve working class men, not separate from them.

Divisions about fighting for liberation are not new. Early in the last century there were arguments between the middle class feminists and working class socialists about whether women's liberation could be achieved within capitalism. As the US socialist Elizabeth Gurley Flynn said in 1915, following a major strike wave involving women workers, 'The sisterhood of women, like the brotherhood of man, is a hollow sham to labour. Behind all its smug hypocrisy and sickly sentimentality loom the sinister outlines of the class war'.[117] The divisions which emerged internationally on class lines then have emerged again now. This article has been mainly concerned with women in Britain but features of their conditions are reproduced across the world as globalisation, imperialism and neo-liberalism make their attacks on working people. If in fighting back against them we make the connection between women's liberation, socialism and the overthrow of class society then we will have brought the possibility of change much closer.

NOTES

1: B Sutcliffe, *100 Ways of Seeing an Unequal World* (London, 2001), p59.

2: www.rapecrisis.co.uk/statistics.htm

3: S Evans, *Personal Politics* (New York, 1979), p190.

4: For the close connection between some of these strikes and the women's movement see *The Body Politic* (London, 1972), pp91-102, 153-174; L German, *Sex, Class and Socialism* (London, 1998), pp163-184; S Rowbotham, *A Century of Women* (London, 1997), pp348-352.

5: See, for example, N Klein, *No Logo* (London, 2001); B Ehrenreich and A Russell Hochschild (eds), *Global Woman* (London, 2003); C Harman, 'The Workers of the World', in *International Socialism* 96 (Autumn 2002); G Horgan, 'How Does Globalisation Affect Women?', *International Socialism* 91 (Summer 2001).

6: A Coote and B Campbell, *Sweet Freedom* (London, 1982), pp74-76.

7: *Financial Times*, 8 February 2001.

8: Figures from *Labour Movement Trends 2001*. See *Financial Times*, 8 February 2001.

9: *Social Trends* 30 (London, 2000), p71.

10: In 1979, 24 percent of such women returned to work, by 1988 this figure stood at 45 percent and in 1996 was at 67 percent (24 percent were full time and 42 percent part time). S Dex (ed), *Families and the Labour Market* (London, 1999), p33.

11: As above, p35.

12: These women's earnings made up 7.9 percent of household income in 1965 and 11.3 percent in 1983. In households where a married woman was working, her income made up 19.5 percent or 27.4 percent of household income, depending on whether there were dependent children or not. See

Jill Walker, 'Women, the State and Family in Britain: Thatcher Economics and the Experience of Women', in J Rubery (ed), *Women and Recession* (London, 1988), p221.

13: D Pilling, 'Engels and the Condition of the Working Class Today', in J Lea and G Pilling (eds), *The Condition of Britain* (London, 1996), p23.

14: S Dex (ed), as above, p42.

15: As above.

16: As above, p43.

17: *Financial Times*, 20 March 2002.

18: L Ward, 'Childcare Gap Stops Mothers Working', *The Guardian*, 26 March 2002.

19: R Bennett, 'Multiplicity Of Childcare Options Fails To Deliver', *Financial Times*, 20 March 2002.

20: R Bennett, 'State May Pay Grandmothers To Baby-Sit', *Financial Times*, 20 March 2002.

21: H Wilkinson, 'The Mother Load', *The Guardian*, 26 March 2002.

22: R Taylor, 'More Women In Paid Employment', *Financial Times*, 8 February 2001.

23: H Wilkinson, as above.

24: R Bennett, 'Multiplicity Of Childcare Options', as above.

25: H Meltzer, *Day Care Services for Children* (a survey carried out on behalf of the Department of Health in 1990) (London, 1994), p19.

26: *Financial Times*, 19 April 2002.

27: H Meltzer, as above, pp56-57.

28: As above, p18.

29: J Rubery and R Tarling, 'Women's Employment in Declining Britain', in J Rubery (ed), as above, pp126-127.

30: *Social Trends* 30 (2000), p72.

31: Demos Report, *Tomorrow's Women*,

1997, quoted in R Coward, *Sacred Cows* (London, 1999), p49.

32: Equal Opportunities Commission figures, quoted in C Palmer, 'Some Still More Equal Than Others', *The Observer*, 11 February 2001 (business section).

33: J Finch, 'Childcare Benefits Count For Nothing', *The Guardian*, 1 March 2001.

34: Hakim's controversial views on this question have been decisively rebutted by various feminist academics. See C Hakim, 'The Myth of Rising Female Employment', in *Work, Employment and Society*, vol 7, no 1 (March 1993), pp97-120; C Hakim, 'Five Feminist Myths about Women's Employment', *British Journal of Sociology*, vol 46, no 3, pp429-455; J Ginn et al, 'Feminist Fallacies: A Reply to Hakim on Women's Employment', *British Journal of Sociology*, vol 47, no 1, pp167-173; I Bruegel, 'Whose Myths are They Anyway?', *British Journal of Sociology* 47 (1), pp175-177; C Hakim, 'The Sexual Division of Labour and Women's Heterogeneity', *British Journal of Sociology*, vol 47, no 1, pp178-188.

35: J Martin and C Roberts, *Women and Employment: A Lifetime Perspective* (London, 1984), chs 3 and 4.

36: S Harkness, 'Working 9 to 5?', in P Gregg and J Wadsworth (eds), *The State of Working Britain* (Manchester, 1999), p106.

37: J Ginn et al, 'Feminist Fallacies', as above, p170.

38: See I Bruegel, as above, p176; Y Cooper, 'How Safe Is Your Job?', *The Independent*, 16 May 1996, which reported that, since 1992, 175,000 more part time workers said they would rather work full time.

39: J Martin and C Roberts, as above, p41.

40: T Desai et al, 'Gender and the Labour Market' in P Gregg and J

Wadsworth (eds), as above, p176.

41: As above, p168.

42: As above, p178.

43: G Gorer, quoted in R McKibbin, *Classes and Cultures: England 1918-1951* (Oxford, 1998), p296.

44: *Social Trends* 30 (2000), p37.

45: As above, p40.

46: *Guardian Education Supplement*, 16 January 2001, p63.

47: 'Battle To Cut Teenage Pregnancy Rate', *The Guardian*, 22 February 2001.

48: J Weeks, *Sex, Politics and Society* (London, 1981), p252.

49: K Wellings et al, *Sexual Behaviour in Britain* (London, 1994), p37.

50: L Stanley, *Sex Surveyed* (London, 1995), p45, quoting survey by Michael Schofield.

51: J Lewis, *Women in Britain since 1945* (Oxford, 1992), p44.

52: C Harman, *The Fire Last Time* (London, 1988), p86.

53: K Wellings et al, as above, pp71-72, shows of those surveyed only 6.1 percent of men and 15.9 percent of women had their first intercourse in marriage, compared with 42.9 percent of men and 51.4 percent of women who had it first in a steady relationship.

54: J Gillis, *For Better, for Worse* (Oxford, 1985), p307.

55: K White, *Sexual Liberation or Sexual License* (Chicago, 2000), p197.

56: J Gillis, as above, pp307-308.

57: K Wellings et al, as above, pp98-100.

58: As above, p77.

59: As above, pp156-157.

60: Figures according to Wellings et al, of those asked about oro-genital sexual contact in the past year, were as follows:

Cunnilingus only: men 6.4 percent, women 5.5 percent
Fellatio only: men 2.7 percent, women 3.3 percent
Both: men 46.5 percent, women 40.7 percent

(K Wellings et al, as above, pp149-151).

61: See, for example, the results of a US study quoted in G Greer, *The Whole Woman* (London, 2000), p241.

62: *US News and World Report*, quoted in G Greer, as above, p234.

63: K Bales, 'Because She Looks Like a Child', in B Ehrenreich and A Russell Hochschild (eds), as above, p219.

64: As above, p214.

65: D Brennan, 'Selling Sex for Visas', in B Ehrenreich and A Russell Hochschild (eds), as above, p157.

66: Quoted in *Metro*, 5 July 2000.

67: Quoted in R Coward, *Sacred Cows* (London, 1999), p75.

68: *Social Trends* 30 (2000), p37.

69: D Hill, 'In Search Of New Dad', *The Guardian*, 14 June 2000.

70: P Hewitt, *About Time* (London, 1993), p58.

71: As above, p57.

72: As above, pp57-58.

73: As above, p61.

74: D Hill, as above.

75: S Dex (ed), as above, p37.

76: www.pbs.org/livelyhood/working family/familytrends.html

77: S Dex (ed), as above, pp38-39, from unpublished tables by E Ferri and K Smith, *Parenting in the 1990s* (London, 1996).

78: S Dex (ed), as above, pp38-39.

79: G Dench, *The Place of Men in Changing Family Cultures* (London, 1996), p63.

80: D Hill, as above.

81: T Blackwell and J Seabrook, *Talking Work: An Oral History* (London, 1996), p141.

82: As above, p161.

83: S Humphries and P Gordon, *A Man's World* (London, 1996), p173.

84: S Nye, 'Act Your Age!', *The Observer Encyclopaedia of Our Times*, vol 1 (London, no date), p3.

85: R Snoddy, 'Staying Active On A Diet Of Sex And Sport', *Financial Times*, 14 April 1997.

86: As above.

87: Letter in *Socialist Review,* January 1997.

88: I Whelehan, *Overloaded* (London, 2000), p65.

89: D Aitkenhead, 'Prudes Rock', *The Guardian*, 5 March 2002.

90: M Phillips, *The Sex Change State* (Social Market Foundation, 1997), p15.

91: As above, p7.

92: S Ruxton, 'Boys Won't be Boys' in T Lloyd and T Wood (eds) *What Next for Men?* (London, 1996), p82.

93: L Brooks, 'Ladies Who Lift', *The Guardian*, 5 March 2002.

94: Quoted in L Segal, *Slow Motion* (London, 1997), p263.

95: *Social Trends* 30 (2000), p58.

96: As above, p56.

97: As above, and A Phillips, 'Down With Girls!', *The Guardian*, 21 June 2000.

98: B Hugill, 'Britain's Exclusion Zone', *The Observer*, 13 April 1997.

99: *Social Trends* 30 (2000), p56.

100: As above, p59.

101: L Rubin, *Families on the Faultline* (New York, 1994), pp112-113.

102: F Engels, *The Condition of the Working Class in England* (Moscow, 1973), p183.

103: As above, p184.

104: As above.

105: F Engels, 'The Origin of the Family, Private Property and the State' in K Marx and F Engels, *Selected Writings* (London, 1968), p461 onwards.

106: For a much more detailed analysis of the women's movement see L German, *Sex, Class and Socialism* (London, 1998).

107: K Roiphe, *The Morning After* (London, 1994), pp52-54.

108: N Wolf, *Fire With Fire* (London, 1993), p318.

109: As above, p48.

110: B Campbell, *Diana, Princess of Wales: How Sexual Politics Shook the Monarchy* (London, 1998), p203.

111: N Klein, as above, p123.

112: As above, p122.

113: See, for example, N Wolf, as above, and R Coward, as above.

114: E Showalter, 'Stop Whingeing, Just Do It', *Financial Times Magazine*, 18 October 2003.

115: B Ehrenreich, 'Maid to Order', in B Ehrenreich and A Russell Hochschild (eds), as above, p90.

116: For a further discussion of the role of the family under capitalism, see L German, *Sex, Class and Socialism* (London, 1998), chapters 1-3.

117: Quoted in M Tax, *The Rising of the Women* (Illinois, 2001), p12.

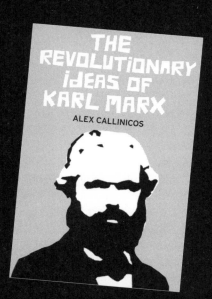

The politics of food
Carlo Morelli

Food has become one of the most important political questions addressed by the anti-capitalist movement. The movement's protests placed agricultural questions at the WTO conferences, in Seattle in 1999 and again in Cancun in 2003, at the centre of the debates that led to the collapse of the meetings. The lack of access to sufficient quantities of food to satisfy minimum human need, referred to as food poverty, the quality of the food we consume and its impact on our health, referred to as food safety, and the control of the world's food resources, known as food security, have all been the focus of attention for many within the growing anti-capitalist movement.

Just a brief look at some of the issues involved explains why this is so. The UN General Assembly stated in 2000 its 'collective responsibility to uphold the principles of human dignity, equality and equity at the global level' and established a series of 'millennium goals' to be achieved by 2015. These included, in the goal of the eradication of extreme hunger, a target of reducing by half the numbers of malnourished people in the world. Yet the UN itself admits that more than 40 countries are not on track to achieve this goal. The extent of food deprivation and threat of famine can be gauged by the fact that overall 36 percent of the population in the least developed countries are officially classed as undernourished. That rises to over 45 percent in those countries on the UN's index of low human development and includes Haiti, Tanzania, Zambia, Congo, Eritrea, Angola, Ethiopia, Mozambique and Burundi. It is still over 40 percent in Tajikistan, Mongolia, Zimbabwe and Kenya, which are officially classed under the

UN's index of medium development countries.[1]

A further measure of extreme poverty comes from the number of people living on less than $1 a day, which has hardly changed in the ten years from 1990 to 2000—1.2 billion people. In sub-Saharan Africa, Latin America and the Caribbean the numbers have actually increased.[2]

Even among those in the developed world with supposedly 'adequate' levels of nutrition, the food we eat has become a major cause of ill health and early death, especially among the poor. Poor diet, alcohol consumption and sedentary lifestyles contribute to 400,000 of the 2 million deaths in the US each year.[3] The levels of obesity, coronary heart disease and diabetes, all diet-related illnesses, are soaring in the US and now across much of the developed world. Levels of obesity in Britain have increased threefold since 1980 and are estimated to reach as high as 30 to 40 percent of the population by 2025, while in the US the rates of obesity could reach 40 to 45 percent of the population.[4] It is suggested that 20,000 people per year die prematurely from diabetes in Britain.[5] Estimates suggest at least 20,000 children have insulin-dependent diabetes in Britain, up from 1,529 diagnosed cases in 1988. One study in Leicester indicated a threefold increase in the number of diagnosed cases in the period from the 1950s to the 1970s.[6]

In Britain we have a society which is eating more, yet what we eat is of lower quality, consisting of high calorie and high fat content foods, leading to diet-related ill health. At the same time high levels of poverty continue to affect large swathes of society. Benzeval, Taylor and Judge's longitudinal study assessing the impact of household income on child development traced the experience of children aged seven until they reached 33 years old. They suggest that children of poor families are twice as likely to develop a longstanding limiting illness as better-off families by the age of 23.[7] Elsewhere Gregg, Harkness and Machin highlighted the 1980s as a period in which income inequality in Britain rose faster than in any other OECD country, leading directly to marked rises in child poverty rates. As a result by 1995-1996 over 4.3 million children, around one in three, were living in households below the poverty line, defined as households whose income is below half the mean household income.[8] It is precisely the poorest in society who consume the foods with the least nutritional quality, and are most likely to develop long term illnesses and die prematurely. Thus the issue of food poverty is explicitly linked to issues of class and the distribution of wealth in both the developed and developing world.

The third point to make is that the food we eat is also directly causing increases in disease and death. Food safety has become a major concern since the food scares of the 1990s and currently over the introduction of genetically modified (GM) crops.

Bovine spongiform encephalopathy (BSE), or mad cow disease, which led to new variant Creutzfeldt-Jakob disease vCJD in humans, has cost over 100 lives so far and it is still feared that as many as 100,000 people may be affected. BSE was publicly linked to vCJD in March 1996 and in the following year some 1.8 million cows and calves were slaughtered, with compensation being paid to farmers and the livestock industry amounting to over £1.5 billion.[9] By 2000 costs had increased to over £4 billion in Britain alone.[10] BSE was believed to have derived from one of two reasons. The official government view was that the mechanical recovery of meat and its reprocessing into animal feed meant that cows were fed the dead remains of other cows leading to the prion protein which caused BSE being rapidly transferred throughout the livestock. Under this view the incidence of BSE in cows should have rapidly died away with the ending of the practice of reprocessing animal remains into animal feeds and the slaughtering of animals born prior to the introduction of these restrictions. However, the continued existence of BSE in Britain, with 1,354 confirmed cases in 2000 and its emergence across Europe, with 329 reported cases in 2000, suggests that BSE may not have been caused by this reprocessing, only spread using reprocessing.[11] The cause of BSE may have been the use of organo–phosphate pesticides on cattle and the feeding of manganese to cattle in order to promote milk production. Under this view the development of the prion protein responsible for BSE derived from the industrial practices used in the cattle industry.[12]

A similar problem emerged with the spread of foot and mouth disease in which the industrialisation of sheep farming, following the concentration of livestock markets and the large distances sheep were transported, led to the rapid spread of infection across much of the British Isles.[13] Thus again it was the changes in the organisation of food production that created the scale of the food scares once disease broke out. Further potential time bombs are also waiting to happen with, for example, E coli infection through the spread of untreated sewage directly onto farmland, whose incidence has increased fourfold from 1990 to

2000.[14]

Finally, concerns over the introduction of GM crops continue. Despite the biotechnology industry's early claims, GM crops are now recognised to cross-pollinate with existing wild species, leading to fears that 'superweeds' could emerge. GM material also inevitably finds its way into the food chain in unpreventable ways. The single field used for the farm-scale crop trial in Fife, Scotland, gave rise to GM material being detected in honey produced two miles away within the first year of the trial.[15] Still more worryingly, GM material has been detected in the human gut, leading to the fear that bacteria may develop which are resistant to antibiotics.[16]

The connection between food poverty, leading to malnutrition in the developing world and ill health in the developed world, lack of food safety, leading to a disease-ridden food chain, and the strong links campaigns have made to the anti-capitalist movement is a recognition that the food industry has played such a major role in creating these outcomes. It has created a system of production which threatens the ability of economies to provide their populations with sufficient quantities of food at sufficient levels of quality to satisfy their needs.[17] Thus it is the undermining of food security and the links between capitalism, food production and big business that lie at the heart of these issues.

Food and big business

We live in a world in which, as with the oil or armaments industries, a few firms dominate the world's food market. Just as the Project for the New American Century provided the ideological explanation for the war against Iraq, so it also provides the ideological explanation of what is now happening to our food. International food policy has been dominated by three interrelated needs: the protection of big business interests and markets in the developed world; the securing of access to raw, unprocessed food products from developing countries; and the securing of access into developing countries' markets for processed exports from the developed world.

One look at the structure of the food industry explains why this is so. For well over 30 years the world food industry has been dominated by the needs of multinational firms, especially those of the US and Britain. By 1974 US and British multinationals were dominating the world's food markets. Of the 100 largest companies 48 were US-owned while a further 22 were British-owned.[18] Currently, of the top 200 companies 100 are US-owned and of the top 50 European companies 19 are British-owned. Together the top 200 food-producing companies in the world account for £700 billion of food sales, or approximately half the world food market, and this share is expected to rise to around two thirds of the market.[19] In Britain three companies—Unilever, Schweppes and Associated British Foods—owned two thirds of total capitalisation of the food industry by 1995. The food industry is one of those few in which British firms still have a strong base. Thus, together with the armaments industry, the British economy can be said to have succeeded in the dubious achievement of creating a competitive advantage in both feeding and killing the world.

An examination of just some of these firms demonstrates the way in which they have secured control over the food industry.

Unilever

Unilever, one of the world's largest food and packaged consumer goods companies, is jointly British and Dutch owned. With worldwide sales of over £30 billion, employing 247,000 workers in over 90 countries in 2002, the company is a truly transnational company. Its origins lie in its development as a soap and margarine manufacturer which later diversified into a wide range of consumer and industrial goods, including even chemicals. This diversification involved developing linkages back to production and transportation as well as forward into manufacturing, distribution and marketing.

Much of Unilever's wealth has come from the exploitation of the developing world, and its origins derive from the advantages it received following the mass clearing of land of indigenous peoples. Unilever's move into plantation ownership and palm oil production in Congo, then a Belgian colony, before the First World War came on the back of the mass destruction of Congolese society. When the contract was signed to hand over up to 200,000 hectares of land the population had reduced from around 40 million down to 8.5 million in the space of 50 years.[20] Such was the importance of these palm oil plantations that Unilever created one of the largest shipping fleets operating out of Africa to bring the oil back to Britain for processing. Through its subsidiaries operating from African countries Unilever was able to dominate trade in unprocessed foodstuffs, controlling 60 percent of palm oil, 45 percent of palm kernel, 60 percent of peanut and 50 percent of cocoa exports from the four British colonies of what are now Nigeria, Ghana, Gambia and Sierra Leone.[21] Even today Unilever continues to have major investments in Africa, with over one fifth of its workforce employed in the African continent. Further, through its Brooke Bond tea company it continues to maintain control over world tea production through its ownership and control of plantations in Kenya and Tanzania as well as India.

The company today has concentrated upon the development of a smaller number of global brands. It boasts 14 brands, each achieving annual sales of over £600 million, including Birds Eye in frozen foods, Dove in soap, Lipton and Brooke Bond in tea and even Calvin Klein in clothing.[22] Finally, despite the company's transnational appearance it remains firmly focused upon the need to influence government policy towards the industry within the developed world. It participates in all the major industrial bodies, including the International Chamber of Commerce along with the more secretive Bilderberg Group, with which the Bush family has close links, as well as British government bodies. These close links are reinforced by the appointment to its board of directors of ex government ministers including Leon Brittan, ex chancellor of the exchequer and trade and industry minister under Margaret Thatcher and European Commissioner from 1989 to 1999, as well as Baroness Chalker, again ex minister for overseas development under Thatcher.

Nestlé

Another multinational company of interest is Nestlé. Nestlé—a Swiss, US and British owned company with turnover exceeding £30 billion—is the manufacturer behind many of the leading chocolate brands such as Kit-Kat. Nestlé gained notoriety for its selling of formula baby milk in Africa which, according to the World Health Organisation, has contributed to the deaths of 1.5 million infants each year from dehydration which, with breast feeding, is largely preventable. Where water is unsafe baby milk fed infants are 25 times more likely to die than breastfed babies. Nevertheless, in 1970 Nestlé executives were stating, on the back of IMF liberalisation policies, that the 'high birth rates [in countries opening up to international trade] permit a rapid expansion in the domain of infant nutrition'. By 1979 the infant formula milk market had become a $2 billion market and by 1998 the market was worth $8 billion. In looking at the African market Nestlé simply applied the processes used in Latin America and East Asia, where in Mexico breastfeeding of six month olds was universal in 1960 but as low as

40 percent by 1966. In Singapore over 80 percent of infants were breastfed in 1951 but by 1971 it was only 5 percent.[23]

The key marketing ploy adopted by Nestlé was to encourage mothers to start feeding their infants artificial baby milk. Once a mother starts with artificial baby milk, and a few days later her milk stops being produced, the infant becomes locked into being fed artificial baby milk. How do you do that? You give away free samples to mothers and provide free or low cost supplies in maternity hospitals and clinics.

Just to prove that a leopard can't change its spots Nestlé was until recently demanding the Ethiopian government compensate the company for the nationalisation of its assets that had occurred in the 1970s. The company demanded $6 million in compensation from the government at a time when it was facing the worst famine since 1984. Only public campaigns by debt groups, including Oxfam, and the sending of 40,000 letters demanding they drop their case forced the company to settle its court action against the Ethiopian government in January 2003.[24]

In the cocoa market—cocoa being the raw material for chocolate— Nestlé has been a major purchaser of cocoa beans. This is an industry heavily dependent upon child labour. UNICEF estimates that as many as one in three children in sub-Saharan Africa below the age of 15 are child workers, of whom some 70 percent work in agriculture.[25] African countries were responsible for over 70 percent of world cocoa production in 2000.[26]

Finally, Nestlé's attitude to labour rights is gauged by its role in the breaking of unions in its plants in Thailand in 1998. Its subcontracted plant in Tedaram became unionised with 13 workers forming the organising committee until Nestlé cut its orders. Nestlé stipulated that lay-offs should follow and include all those on the organising committee before orders would increase. As a result the unionisation of the plant collapsed.

Both Unilever and Nestlé are typical of the large agribusinesses that have emerged to dominate the world food industry. Originally creating a highly vertically integrated structure, owning the farms and plantations along with the processing and distribution firms, large firms capable of fixing prices and output in order to maximise profits have dominated the industry. As they have developed they have begun to move away from direct ownership of the farms themselves and have instead concentrated on the 'value adding' processing of raw foodstuffs. In so doing they have consciously acted to ensure raw material prices are kept at a minimum. An important mechanism in keeping raw material prices low is control over the supply chain. In the cocoa industry, for instance, although Africa produces around 70 percent of world output it is responsible for only around 12 percent of processing. Europe, particularly the Netherlands, France, Britain and Germany, is responsible for around 45 percent of world processing of cocoa.[27] Large multinationals also benefit from the development of horizontal integration in their operations. Operating not simply in single product lines but across the full range of food processes and markets, large firms are again able to gain still greater influence in related markets.

Sainsbury's

One further aspect of the domination of the food industry by large firms that requires examination is the concentration in food retailing. Food retailing has increasingly become dominated by large integrated food distribution firms. The British retailer Sainsbury's and four other retailers control as much as 90 percent of the food market in Britain. They have achieved this dominance through building chains of large stores, as large as 100,000 square feet, linked to a network of distribution centres and logistics firms delivering goods in a just-in-time system rivalling anything in the manufacturing sector. These large stores with as many as 20,000 different products, we are told, give us choice and low prices. Yet the reality is very different.

The choices we get are increasingly between the same product packaged in different ways, literally in the case of many own-labels and manufacturer brands. It is a 'choice' which imposes standards of uniformity on produce whose aim is to maximise the company's ability to increase the throughput of products. This means that perfectly good produce is left to rot in fields and on farms because it is the wrong colour or wrong shape, or has some minor blemish. As a result foods are grown and species bred simply for their ability to produce uniform products rather than their taste or nutritional qualities.

Still more damaging are the environmental results of this system of food production. The centralisation of distribution means that our food travels huge distances and the environmental consequences of this travel are borne by consumers in higher pollution levels, increases in greenhouse gas emissions and expenditure on road networks that subsidises the costs of transportation to the retailing firms. As many as 30 percent of lorry journeys are accounted for by empty vehicles, a figure that has remained constant over the past ten years.[28] Seven percent of road vehicles are HGVs, yet they produce 22 percent of carbon dioxide pollution, 32 percent of nitrogen oxide pollution and 42 percent of fine particulate pollution. The food industry is directly responsible for much of this, contributing 40 percent of the increase in goods vehicle movements on our roads.[29] The external costs of road transportation have been estimated at around 4.7 percent of GDP for the UK in 1991.[30] Thus there are substantial hidden costs to the food production system currently in place which add to the costs of our food but are paid for indirectly by consumers.

Localisation

One response to the problems identified above has been the call for more localised food production, with locally sited production aimed at smaller local markets. Localisation, giving governments the ability to subsidise domestic production in the developing world, could, it is argued (in the food industry, if not manufacturing), enhance food security, reduce the control exercised by multinational companies over national markets and reduce environmental costs of production as less intensive production methods are introduced.[31]

The promotion of farmers' markets in Britain has been one manifestation of these ideas.[32] The reduction in food miles (the distance food products are transported) and the resultant reduction in pollution would of course be welcome. Similarly, the ability of developing economies to have greater food security, reducing the risk of famine, would equally be a major improvement for hundreds of millions of the world's population. Leaving aside the general criticism of the localisation thesis—that no economy can develop in isolation from the rest of the world economy, with levels of investment, human capital and economies of scale such that specialisation is essential for economic growth—calls for localisation of food production confuse two essential issues.

The central problem in the food system is one of exploitation of small producers and landless labourers by more powerful groups of firms. It is not one primarily of the geography of this exploitation. The inequalities in the relations of production are not resolved by calls for localisation, rather they are created at a more local level. The movement away from direct ownership by the largest multinationals of farming facilities is one indication of this. The market control they seek is through the domination of supply chains and processing. It is here that they believe 'value adding' and product differ-entiation can be achieved. One example of this is provided by the sale of fair trade goods by the large supermarkets. Fair trade is a system developed to ensure primary producers of products receive a higher level of payment for their goods. The supermarkets are able to pay higher prices for fair trade goods because they pass on this premium to consumers in the form of higher prices. Thus it is consumers, not big business, who bear the cost of fair trade products.

In reality then it is the control over the supply chain that allows big businesses to capture the value created by the labour of peasants and small farmers, as well as capture the value created in the processing of raw food-stuffs by the workers they employ. Neither do moves towards more sustainable production, such as organic production, fundamentally challenge the dominance of large transnational companies. Indeed, the largest transna-tional food corporations, such as Unilever, have proved adept at responding to rising demand for organic production in the developed world. Unilever has recently bought the Scotland-based organic food producer Go Organic Ltd as it responded to the new opportunities in higher value added sectors such as organic foods, while retailers such as Sainsbury's and Tesco have expanded their range of organic and locally produced products. Worse still, the expansion of demand for organic foods in the developed world has increased the food miles as a result of the very high levels of imports, cur-rently around 70 percent of produce, required to satisfy rising demand.

Thus the criticism made about the dominant market position these companies have created is not one of size or integration per se. Rather it is about the use this power is put to. It is the exploitation of workers and peasant farmers in the food industries, the underdevelopment of poorer nations and exploitation of consumers that this power permits that is the problem.

Locating the rise of globalisation as the cause of the problems of food poverty, food safety and food security suggests that prior to the rise of these multinational conglomerates there was some 'golden age' of food production. The reality is the opposite. The growth of world food produc-tion has occurred alongside the growth of these corporations. While the 'green revolution' which took place after the Second World War has brought with it a move towards monoculture farming and unsustainable industrialised techniques, it nevertheless ensured that no link between population growth and food supplies emerged. The last half of the 20th century saw population growth at historic levels, yet per capita food production outpaced this growth.[33] The Malthusian theory suggesting food supplies would be outstripped by population growth was decisively rejected. Since the Second World War the problem of food supplies has always been of oversupply, dumping and the maldistribution of existing supplies rather than one of inadequate production and scarcity. This should not be any surprise to Marxists. Capitalist accumulation has ensured that firms compete with one another to gain market share and a monopolistic control over each industry. In the process innovation and investment occur which expand productive capacity, until there is too much output to be absorbed in the market and a crisis of 'overproduction' occurs. That a crisis of 'overproduction' can occur while people starve is one extreme example of the destructive tendencies within capitalism. The food industry has been particularly prone to these anarchic capitalist cycles and it is exactly these crises that have led it, as an industry, to seek levels of government intervention to regulate the market that no other industry has achieved.

So the question of size is linked to one of power. This can be seen most clearly when we examine how the market for food is structured and how the companies themselves and the key individuals within these companies play a dominant role in directing these institutions.

Subsidies and trade

The development of large transnational firms has given rise to a system of production whereby their size and dominance have provided them with an ability to structure the food market. Characteristic of this system of production are high levels of vertical co-operation in which close linkages between large-scale farmers, manufacturers and retailers are used to regulate competition. The key players in the industry are the manufacturers and the retailers who dominate the individual sectors and in doing so attempt to determine the prices and profits in the industry as a whole. Most of these companies operate as dominant firms in their respective market sectors. That provides them with the opportunities to establish prices and profits within the supply chain and ensure governments introduce rules which benefit them and help them dominate small producers. We can see this when we examine how prices are actually determined.

Neo-liberal ideology suggests that prices are determined by the interaction of demand and supply. In the food industry nothing could be further from the truth. Farmers receiving subsidies provide manufacturers and retailers with the ability to purchase low-priced raw materials and sell them at high prices to consumers. A system of import tariffs and subsidisation from governments provides subsidies throughout the industry and then on top of these consumers pay high prices for the food they buy. This system emerged across the developed world and has been established ever since the collapse of the unregulated markets before the First World War. In the British case initial price supports emerged with the outbreak of the First World War but became firmly entrenched with the Import Duties Act of 1932, the Agricultural Marketing Acts of 1931 and 1933 and the Wheat Act of 1932. After the Second World War the Agricultural Act of 1947 intensified this system and entry into the Common Market with the Common Agricultural Policy (CAP) became the method after 1973. It is important to realise, therefore, that the methods of subsidisation and support for agriculture date back almost a century and CAP is simply the latest progression in this process. But what is the role of these subsidies?

CAP, the common agricultural policy of the EU, has been suggested to be a policy aimed at protecting small farmers, especially in France, and thus wedding them to right wing ideology in the face of an emerging cold war within Europe.[34] However, CAP is also a system aimed at increasing productivity, stabilising farm income, stabilising market prices and finally ensuring the maintenance of supplies. The thrust of CAP is to encourage production of agricultural products and it has encouraged a continued decline in the numbers of agricultural workers and small farmers. As a result, the £20 billion spent annually on CAP goes in production subsidies and price supports. Hence the bulk of the subsidies goes to the larger farmers, not the small farmers.[35]

CAP also ensures two further developments. First, agricultural imports from outside the EU face a high common tariff. These tariffs increase—a ramping effect—the more processed these imports are. So agricultural imports from the developing world will tend to be raw materials and unprocessed goods, such as for cocoa as described above. This has the impact of preventing industrialisation in the developing world. Second, CAP's success in promoting production-based agriculture has left the EU with large quantities of agricultural products which cannot be sold in the

EU without reducing prices. As a result CAP has introduced export subsidies, which has encouraged the dumping of products in markets outside the EU. So, for example, beef produced in the EU could be bought in South Africa at 30 pence a kilo while it cost £1 a kilo to produce it.[36] These export subsidies have the effect of undermining agricultural producers in the developing world. Of course once domestic competitors are eliminated, fluctuations in world market prices lead directly to rising food prices in the developing world.

Food multinationals are also able to determine the structure of the food system through the regulation of international trade in raw materials and processed foods. Again this can be traced back to the breakdown of international trade after the First World War, but was most clearly established with the post Second World War institutions of the World Bank, the IMF, GATT and its successors the World Trade Organisation and, most importantly, the 1993 Agreement on Agriculture.

The opening up of economies to trade which the General Agreement on Trade and Tariffs (GATT) promoted and the IMF's approach to industrialisation through an export market led orientation on cash crops have, since the 1970s, been instrumental in promoting famine. They have undermined both food security (the ability of a country to provide adequate levels of nourishment for its population) and food sovereignty (the ability of governments to determine the way in which that food is produced and distributed). In the period between 1970 and 1981 imports of agricultural products into developing economies rose three times faster than exports, such that by 1981 developing countries exporting agricultural products had become net importers and Africa's share of markets for agricultural goods in the developed world fell from 8.5 percent to 3.7 percent.[37] More recently, in 2002 the IMF dictated to governments such as Malawi that it sell its emergency food reserves on world markets, in order to ensure its debt repayments were made, just as the country faced its worst famine since 1949.[38]

Most starkly, a look at the Agreement on Agriculture demonstrates how big business interests dominate the processes of trade and development. The Agreement on Agriculture emerged from the Uruguay round of GATT negotiations in 1993, the same negotiations that launched the WTO. The agreement had three key points: to increase market access, to reduce export subsidies and finally to reduce domestic support for agriculture. Governments agreed to reduce tariffs on imports and permit a minimum access of 5 percent in each market sector. The result of this has been that once multinationals have been able to gain access to even a small proportion of the market they have used their market power to drive out local producers. The UN Food and Agriculture Organisation's 1999 study demonstrated that countries implementing the Agreement on Agriculture saw a surge of food imports but no increase in exports. Of 16 developing countries only Thailand saw an increase in exports. Estimates suggest that at least 20 to 30 million small peasant farmers have been driven from the land in recent years as a result.[39] Not surprisingly, no increase in exports into the US and EU occurred because the agreement accepted that these areas had reduced their subsidies in line with the agreement prior to its introduction. Despite the fact that subsidies in Western countries rose from $182 billion in 1995 to $362 billion in 1998 these markets remained closed to developing economies' exports.[40]

The agreement also encouraged the longstanding policy of the IMF and the World Bank to encourage developing economies to shift production from food for the local economy to export-aimed cash crops. So large areas of Indian agricultural land previously used for food production, including in Andra Pradesh, Karnataka and West Bengal, have been taken over for the production of fresh flowers and cotton for export markets such as Europe. The result is that much of the most fertile land is taken out of food production, peasant farmers are impoverished and the profits deriving from large-scale business are reaped by multinationals, leaving populations with fewer resources to purchase imported food and economies less able to produce enough food to feed their populations.

So a system of production emerges which protects large-scale producers in domestic markets through a system of subsidies and tariff protection and at the same time favours big business interests internationally through the creation of export subsidies and rules demanding increased market access. When we look at the connections between big business and government the reason for these developments also becomes crystal clear.

A close interconnection has emerged between business, international organisations and government such that the distinction between politicians and business men and women has almost disappeared. As mentioned above, Unilever has been keen to appoint ex government ministers onto its board. Similarly, with Nestlé the interests of the board of directors demonstrate the close links between business and the regulation of competition and trade. Nestlé's chairman, Helmut Maucher, also serves as a board member of Bayer, one of the major companies behind attempts to introduce GM crops. He is also a member of the Board of Trustees of the World Economic Forum and chair of the International Chamber of Commerce, both of which play a leading role in the WTO discussions on international trade. Arthur Dunkel, another Nestlé director, was in fact director-general of GATT until 1993 and was a member of the WTO disputes panel as well as being a member of the International Chamber of Commerce working group on international trade and investment policy.

Within Britain the largest retailing firms have systematically developed closer connections between themselves. A recent study demonstrated that 90 percent of the 20 largest retailers in Britain share directors with other related firms compared with 50 percent in 1975. The number of multiple directorships held has quadrupled in the same period to 34 percent.[41]

A series of close connections and interrelationships exist between the largest firms in the food industry and international institutions for the regulation of trade and governments in the developed world. These reinforce a series of financial supports developed to protect and stabilise the food industry. These relationships, however, are themselves not new. Lenin identified these close linkages between the state and monopoly capitalism and similarly connected the development of monopoly capitalism with imperialist exploitation and war.[42] Many of the connections Lenin identified are, as already described, readily seen today in the food industry. The process of globalisation, through the Agreement on Agriculture, has brought these relationships into the open more clearly than was previously the case.

The fact that these relationships are so clearly exposed requires not simply an explanation for their origins but also conclusions pointing to ways in which these relationships should be challenged and broken. This article started by making a connection between food poverty, food safety and food security. Any alternatives clearly need to be measured against their impact in these three areas.

Conclusions

The most important point to reiterate is that there is currently the ability to produce enough food to adequately feed the world's population. The primary problem facing the developing world is the distribution of food and its control. While there are demands for greater food security and greater access to developed world markets from producers in the developing world, until the chains of exploitation are broken these demands will, at best, only be realised in so far as they provide the major businesses with new business opportunities. In other words the mechanism used for the integration of the developing world will be one which ensures the continued system of exploitation of the majority of peasants and workers producing food for the world's populations. The geography of exploitation may change but the relations of exploitation will remain. Yet it seems unlikely that even this limited restructuring of the world food industry will occur given the interests at stake in the developed world.

In the absence of any such fundamental change in the relations of production it is still necessary to recognise that food security has become a major issue for the developed and developing world. The US and British governments are desperate to ensure that the control over the world's food resources is firmly within the grip of firms they are linked with. Both the ability of developing countries to feed their populations to an adequate level and their ability to determine how that food is produced and distributed within their economies must again be a starting point for any debate. Any moves, such as freer trade, which undermine food security or sovereignty must be a step away from increasing equality. The origins of the problems of food security and sovereignty derive from the anarchy of a market which, despite the role played by Western governments, sees prices fluctuate wildly causing famine. Only a planned rational production system in which investment in agriculture and food production was not duplicated across the globe causing overproduction could guarantee equality.

Should we seek to move away from industrial farming systems? Here the concern is that current farming techniques, factory-produced meat, and fertiliser-reliant techniques for crop production are unsustainable in terms of wasting the earth's resources and damaging the environment. Certainly we should seek methods of production which are sustainable, but that does not rule out all industrial forms of agriculture. There is not a simple dichotomy between non-organic and organic farming—rather a continuum exists between the two. Certainly moves away from monoculture farming heavily dependent upon chemical fertilisers and herbicides is necessary. Nevertheless, this does not dictate the adoption of fully organic production. Food security and an end to food poverty are the essential criteria, and in so far as alternative farming techniques achieve the same goals they should be welcomed because of their sustainability.

Capitalism has created the conditions in which commodities can be transported around the world. Specialisation in production has been beneficial and can be more efficient for many products. However, in agriculture the extent of these economies of scale is open to question. Specialisation in the form of monoculture farming encourages the spread of disease, increases chemical costs and can result in lower yields.[43] Further, the true extent of efficiency of current farming is hidden behind governments' cross-subsidisation of production and accounting techniques which ignore externalities caused by pollution and transportation. Nevertheless, replacing subsidies for large-scale farming with subsidising local production does not in and of itself represent any advance for humankind. Equally it is certainly the case that economies of scale are more easily identified in the processing of food. In any rational world we would not wish to see chocolate produced in hundreds of thousands of small plants when it is more efficient to build larger plants capable of dealing with the quantities necessary to cater for demand. Therefore, the issue is the extent to which food sufficiency, safety and security can be achieved in a sustainable way and in a way which disentangles the questions of market power and underdevelopment from production.

To conclude, the debate between localisation and globalisation in food production needs to start from considerations of satisfying human need rather than a value judgement on the benefits or otherwise of rival systems. Any rational food production system would certainly lead to higher levels of localised production, certainly to greater diversity in the food we consume and certainly not a world in which millions starve while food is left to rot. Neither would a rational food production system see millions being made ill from the poor quality of the food produced or a world in which the food produced was determined by the needs of big business to maximise profits. But equally, with a world population of 6 billion, it would almost certainly involve the continuation of some forms of large-scale agricultural production and international trade in food, but at a level which is sustainable, rational and aimed at satisfying the needs of all.

NOTES

1: UN, *Human Development Report 2002: Deepening Democracy in a Fragmented World* (Oxford, 2002), p17 and table 7.

2: As above, table 1.2.

3: M Nestle, *Food Politics: How the Food Industry Influences Nutrition and Health* (Berkley, 2002), p7.

4: T Lang and G Raynor (eds), *Why Health is the Key to the Future of Food and Farming* (London, 2002), p28 and figure 7.

5: M MacKinnon, *Providing Diabetes Care in General Practice: A Practical Guide for the Primary Care Team*, 3rd edn (London, 1998), p24.

6: British Diabetic Association, *Diabetes in the UK* (London, 1995), p9.

7: M Benzeval, J Taylor and K Judge, 'Evidence on the Relationship between Low Income and Poor Health: Is the Government Doing Enough?', *Fiscal Studies* 21:3 (2000), pp375-399.

8: P Gregg, S Harkness and S Machin, 'Poor Kids: Trends in Child Poverty in Britain, 1968-96', *Fiscal Studies* 20:2 (1999), pp163-187.

9: DTZ Consulting, *The Economic Impact of BSE on the UK Economy* (Manchester, 1998), table 5.1.

10: T Lang and G Raynor, as above, p39.

11: DEFRA, *BSE: Weekly Cumulative Stats*, http://www.maff.gov.uk/animalh/bse/bse-statistics/level-4-weekly-stats.html includes confirmed cases and confirmed cases not placed under restriction, and Office International Des Epizooties, *Number of Reported Cases of BSE Worldwide (excluding the United Kingdom)*, http://www.oie.int/eng/info/en_esbmonde.htm

12: G Monbiot, 'Mad Cows are Back', *BBC Wildlife Magazine*, April 2001.

13: C Morelli, 'Food Scare: Enough to Make You Sick', *Socialist Review* 251 (April 2001), p22.

14: T Lang and G Raynor, as above, figure 2.

15: *The Scotsman*, 16 September 2002.

16: M W Ho, 'Stacking the Odds Against Finding It', *Science in Society*, 16 (2002), p28.

17: The term 'system of production' helps to focus attention on the interconnectedness of the food industry. See B Fine, *The Political Economy of Diet, Health and Food Policy* (London, 1998).

18: J Burns, 'A Synoptic View of the Food Industry', in J Burns, J McInerney and A Swinbank (eds), *The Food Industry: Economics and Policies* (London, 1983), p11.

19: T Lang, 'The Complexities of Globalisation: The UK as a Case of Tensions within the Food System and the Challenge to Food Policy' (Thames Valley University, 1999), quoted in C Hines, *Localisation: A Global Manifesto* (London, 2000), p103.

20: B Dinham and C Hines, *Agribusiness in Africa: A Study of the Impact of Big Business on Africa's Food and Agricultural Production* (London, 1983), p167.

21: Corporate Watch, 'Unilever, a Truly Multi-local Multinational' (2001), p26, www.corporatewatch.org.uk

22: Unilever, *Annual Report & Accounts*, 2003, p6.

23: See M Brady, 'Foods for Infants: How the Baby Food Industry Competes with Breastfeeding', in J Madeley (ed), *Hungry for Power* (London, 1999) pp8-15.

24: C Denny, 'Nestlé U-Turn On Ethiopia Debt', *The Guardian*, 24 January 2003.

25: UNICEF, www.unicef.org/protection/index_childlabour.html

26: International Cocoa Organisation (ICCO), *2001 Annual Report*, table 1.

27: ICCO, as above, table 2.

28: Estimates of light running vehicles, ie those which are not fully loaded, are still higher. DETR, *Sustainable Distribution: A Strategy* (London, 1999), p2.

29: DETR, as above, pp3-4.

30: D Maddison et al, *The True Costs of Road Transport* (London, 1996) Box A1, p220.

31: See C Hines, *Localisation: A Global Manifesto*, as above.

32: As above, pp210-218.

33: P Foster, *The World Food Problem: Tackling the Causes of Undernutrition in the Third World* (London, 1992), pp172-173.

34: A S Milward, *The European Rescue of the Nation-State* (London, 1992).

35: P Allanson, 'CAP Reform and the Distribution of Farm Income in Scotland', *University of Dundee Economics Discussion Papers*, 147 (2003).

36: J Madeley, *Hungry for Trade* (London, 2000), p71. It should also be noted that it was claimed that foot and mouth entered into Britain from infected meat from Africa. While this might have been a racist myth, if it is true it may well be that the meat originated from the EU in the first place.

37: UN Food and Agriculture Organisation, *The State of Food and Agriculture 1984* (Rome, 1985), p54.

38: E Burgo and H Stewart, 'IMF Policies "Led To Malawi Famine"', *The Guardian*, 29 October 2002.

39: J Madeley, *Hungry for Trade*, as above, pp73-75.

40: As above, p45.

41: A B Thomas, 'The Changing Structure of Intercorporate Relations Among Britain's Largest Retail Firms', *Service Industries Journal* 22 (2002), p29.

42: V I Lenin, *Imperialism: The Highest Stage of Capitalism* (Beijing, 1975).

43: See G Monbiot, 'Organic Farming Will Feed The World', *The Guardian*, 24 August 2000, for a review, and P Rosset, 'Cuba: A Successful Case Study of Sustainable Agriculture', in F Magdoff, J Bellamy Foster and F Buttel (eds), *Hungry for Profit* (New York, 2000).

*Libel*appeal

This is an appeal to all socialists and free thinkers to contribute to the enormous costs of a case brought against socialists by socialists.

In August last year, the editor of *Socialist Review*, Lindsey German, and Bookmarks Publications, the socialist publisher, got a letter from the well known libel lawyers Peter Carter-Ruck and Partners on behalf of their clients Quintin Hoare and Branca Magas.

The letter complained about an article written in 1993 by Alex Callinicos (who also got a letter) and included in the book *The Balkans, Nationalism and Imperialism*, published in 1999 by Bookmarks.

The details of the complaint were spelled out in a statement read in open court recently.

Hoare and Magas complained that one passage in the article meant they were both 'apologists' for Franjo Tudjman and his regime in Croatia.

This letter is not concerned with the allegations in the original publication. It has been a long tradition in the labour movement that arguments between socialists should be conducted openly and should not, except in extreme circumstances, be tested in the courts by the libel laws.

The reason for this tradition is simple. As soon as lawyers get involved in these arguments, the expense of the action in almost every case far exceeds both any damage done by the libel and anything a socialist publisher or author can possibly afford.

This history of this case vindicates that tradition. Quintin Hoare and Branca Magas are well known in British left wing circles. From the outset Bookmarks Publications and Lindsey German made no attempt to justify their article. They sought to settle the matter as soon and as cheaply as possible.

After much correspondence they agreed to make a statement in open court apologising for the article and agreeing to pay each of the plaintiffs £1,500. Carter-Ruck's bill for these proceedings is likely to be over £10,000.

This means that the total bill for bringing the action and pursuing it, though it was undefended, is more than three times the payment made to the two people who made the complaint. And this for an item in a book whose total sale at Bookmarks and other bookshops in the year before the complaint was less than 50!

At no stage did Mr Hoare or Ms Magas approach Bookmarks Publications without their lawyers. They went straight to their lawyers, at no expense to themselves, since Carter-Ruck were operating on a "no win, no fee" basis.

Bookmarks Publications is a small left wing publisher with very few funds, all of which go into developing new publications. The publisher, Lindsey German and Alex Callinicos cannot possibly afford these sums.

Hence this appeal to anyone in the socialist and labour movement who would like to express their disapproval of pursuing political arguments through the law courts.

Paul Foot

Please make donations payable to Bookmarks Libel Fund and send to 1 Bloomsbury Street, London WC1B 3QE. Donations by debit and credit card can be taken by phone on 020 7637 1848 or e-mail publications@bookmarks.uk.com

In the middle way[1]
Colin Barker

A review of Geoff Eley, **Forging Democracy: The History of the Left in Europe, 1850–2000** *(Oxford University Press, 2002), £25*

In 1985 Geoff Eley, with David Blackbourn, co-authored *The Peculiarities of German History*. That book represented an important contribution to Marxist thinking, not just about 19th century German history, but about how we should understand 'bourgeois revolutions'.[2] In the intervening years Eley has produced a steady flow of articles and books on the history of Germany, the working class, popular culture, and the work of prominent Marxists like Christopher Hill and Edward Thompson. It was thus with some anticipation that I opened his 698-page book, dealing with the interlinked themes of the development of democracy and of the left in Europe over the past century and a half.

The author tells us that he produced this volume over the last 20 years. He was writing during the 1980s and 1990s, in a period that significantly reshaped the European and world left, when it was peculiarly difficult for socialists to maintain their bearings. The events of that period—the large defeats suffered by centrally important groups like the Italian Fiat workers or the British miners, the rise and fall of various parliamentary and extraparliamentary left movements including the 1980s peace movement, the apparent prominence of 'new social movements', the collapse of 'communism' in Eastern Europe and the former USSR, and the drive towards neo-liberalism by the parties of social democracy (and above all the Blair-led New Labour Party)—could easily depress socialists or lead them astray. Certainly the sense they made of those decades necessarily informed how they thought about the history of their own movements. As he acknowledges, Geoff Eley has been marked by the period of his own research and writing. The views he formed then have shaped his history.

Any serious review of this ambitious book must, therefore, be political. If I locate serious problems in *Forging Democracy*, my argument is almost entirely not with Eley's 'facts', but with the pattern he has found in them, the lessons he has drawn, and the issues he has emphasised as well as those he has neglected. On a number of critical matters, there are major differences between Eley and the tradition broadly represented by this journal.

Themes

There are several repeating themes running through Eley's book. On the first of these we can open with agreement. Between 1860 and 2000, as Eley suggests:

> ...the most important gains for democracy have only ever been attained through revolution, or at least via those several concentrated periods of change I'll call the constitution-making conjunctures of modern European history.[3] Let there be no mistake: democracy is not 'given' or 'granted'. It requires *conflict*, namely, courageous challenges to authority, risk-taking and reckless exemplary acts, ethical witnessing, violent confrontations, and general crises in which the given sociopolitical order breaks down. In Europe, democracy did not arise from natural evolution or economic prosperity. It certainly did not emerge as an inevitable by-product of individualism or the market. It developed because masses of people organised collectively to demand it.[4]

To this we should add that democracy in Europe has also been a fragile, contested, unfinished and relatively recent growth. Not only have democratic advances occurred via major political crises, so too have the sometimes crushing defeats which the struggle for democracy in Europe has experienced: think only of the victories of Mussolini, Hitler or Franco between the wars, of Stalinist reaction across Eastern Europe after 1945, or the Greek colonels' coup.

There have, Eley argues, been five moments in European history of 'transnational constitution-making', each of which laid down possibilities and limits for decades afterwards. The first, 1789-1815, lies outside his book's remit. The other four were 1869-1871, 1914-1923, 1943-1949, and 1989-1992[4]. In practice, Eley doesn't hold very firmly to this list, spending some space, for example, in considering the 'political explosions of 1968'. But his general argument is surely right: history moves between periods when nothing fundamental seems to change and when politics seems to become 'the machinery of maintenance and routine', and other periods when:

> ...things fall apart. The given ways no longer persuade. The present loosens its grip. Horizons shift. History speeds up. It becomes possible to see the fragments and outlines of a different way. People shake off their uncertainties and hesitations; they throw aside their features. Very occasionally, usually in the midst of a wider societal crisis, the apparently unbridgeable structures of normal political life become shaken. The expectations of a slow and unfolding habitual future get unlocked. Still more occasionally, collective agency materialises, sometimes explosively and with violent results. When this happens, the formal institutional worlds of politics in a nation or a city and the many mundane worlds of the private, the personal and the everyday move together. They occupy the same time. The present begins to move. These are times of extraordinary possibility and hope. New horizons shimmer. History's continuum shatters.[5]

We need not discuss here how and why such dramatic shifts in tempo and possibility occur, what matters is that they do happen. Leaps and jumps in development, political and social crises, unexpected transformations are *normal* in history, and they affect the way that socialists, above all, respond to the past, the present and the future.

The other recurring themes present some difficulties, which we shall need to pick up at appropriate points. One concerns gender and class. Left politics, Eley suggests, has been centred around 'the traditional imagery of the male worker in industry'[6] and this imagery has weakened the left both theoretically and strategically. Several problems arise. The European left's approach to what an earlier generation termed 'the woman question' has, he proposes, been consistently flawed, so that the very term 'class' itself has been identified in 'masculine' terms. In practice this has often weakened the left's assessment of and struggle for democratic advance. Additionally, Eley suggests that the 'centrality of the working class' has been 'deconstructed' in contemporary social and economic thought, and this leads him to ask what happens if we 'dethrone' the working class from its privileged primacy in socialist politics at various periods in the past? In this, he draws inspiration from 'feminist critiques of "class-centred" politics', as these developed in the 1970s.[7]

There's a second, problematic theme concerning Eley's account of what some rather critical terms—notably 'the left' and 'socialism'—should be taken to mean, and what and who should be included in and excluded from them. These issues were, of course, themselves very much contested across Europe during the period covered by *Forging Democracy*, and the author's own stance with respect to these debates cannot but affect his historical treatment.

There's a final theme, although it is not openly stated in the introductory pages. Faced with a variety of crises, in which the left found itself divided and arguing furiously, Eley's instinct is to seek some middle path between the contending forces. Closely connected with this, not surprisingly, is Eley's generally unsympathetic rendering of the Leninist tradition, and indeed a not very convincing account of the politics of Marxism generally.

This review will follow the broad organisation of Eley's book into four sections.

1860-1914

The 1860s represent a useful starting point for the history of the left and democracy in Europe. The decade saw a series of state reorganisations across the world, whose effects would be felt for the next century. Serfdom was abolished 'from above' in Tsarist Russia, Italy and Germany were unified from above, Canada gained its federal constitution, the North won the Civil War in America and abolished slavery, and the Meiji Restoration set Japan on the path to rapid capitalist development. The British parliament, through the Second Reform Act and the Education Act, gave some male workers the vote and provided for a national state education system. All the major states which were to play prominent roles as Great Powers in inter-imperialist conflicts in the 20th century underwent significant political changes between 1860 and 1870.

The formation of unified and relatively liberalised national states was, as Eley notes, a necessary preliminary to the struggle for democracy. It was in the new world of large nation-states in late 19th century Europe that modern socialist movements emerged. As industrial capitalism and its system of states developed, so too did the content of popular demands for democracy:

> Gradually and unevenly, democracy became linked to two new demands: an economic analysis of capitalism and a political programme for the general reorganising of society. The new ideas didn't inevitably follow from socio-economic change. But in the most general way, changes in the democratic idea clearly had this material source. They resulted from the serious efforts of political thinkers, and countless ordinary men and women, to understand the disruptions of their accustomed world. It was in that moment of transformation that people began exploring the possibilities of collective ownership and co-operative production. And in that juncture of socioeconomic change and political rethinking the ideas of socialism were born.[8]

In that process, the prefix 'social' was attached to 'democracy' to define a distinctive working class politics. And the term 'social democracy' implied a new form of society, contrasted sharply with emerging capitalism: 'It came to mean "an idea of society as mutual cooperation", as opposed to one based on "individual competition".'[9] Private property itself came to be identified as the source of social ills.

Two intimately interlinked questions were naturally posed. First, how should this new social democratic vision be realised? Second, what content should be given to this vision?

So far as the first question was concerned, the predominant solution adopted across Europe involved the creation of new, social democratic parties. These, Eley suggests, displaced older forms: notably local workers' associations and clubs on the one hand, and 'Blanquism' on the other. Where they were successful, the new parties absorbed workers' associations, around a new project. If only working people could gain the vote, then universal suffrage should permit a parliamentary majority to institute social democratic change. The newly emerging socialist parties were a realisation of a broad democratic vision, which focused working class political energies on parliamentary politics.

Looking back from the early 21st century, it seems improbable that such a project could catch fire with millions of people. Plenty of people today think politics is restricted to parliamentarism, but true believers in 'parliamentary socialism', who still seriously see this as a means to uproot the whole social foundation of capitalism, are quite few. In that sense, someone like Tony Benn is relatively unusual. But before 1914 such ideas could enjoy wide appeal. Nor is this surprising. In the 19th century most male workers were still excluded from the suffrage, as of course were all women. What could be more natural than the assumption that, if the ruling class denied you the vote, acquiring it could be a powerful means to both oppose them and remake society?

Eley mostly interprets the growth of social democratic parties as a 'forward march of labour'. He is, surely, broadly correct in his positive presentation of the 'socialist model of the mass party, campaigning openly for public support and parliamentary representation on a national scale, and organising its own affairs by the internal democracy of meetings, resolutions, agreed procedures, and elected committees'. This was 'the crucial democratic breakthrough of the 19th century's last four decades'—it was 'the *vital* departure'.[10]

There is, however, a curious gap in his story, in that he does not pay much attention to the interrelation between the pursuit of parliamentary victories and questions of trade unionism and workplace struggle. The pre-1914 decades witnessed a considerable growth in union membership and activity across Europe, in part absorbing the forces which were previously drawn into 'workers' associations'. As both national trade union structures and the social democratic parties grew, they fostered each other's development. (The patterns of development, though, did not follow the same order in each country. While the Labour Party in Britain was largely the creation of the unions, in Germany the order was reversed.) In a book focused on the relation between the left and democracy, Eley's relative inattention to trade unionism—which marks his whole book—means that he never very directly addresses the complex of theoretical and practical issues about struggles over authority and thus democracy within the capitalist workplace. Yet the 'despotic' power of employers and their managerial apparatus, from bullying, racist and sexist supervisors to the 'scientific' managers who tried to squeeze ever more surplus value from workers, were as much a source of trade unionism's attraction as questions of wages alone. The struggle to control the exercise of capitalist power in and around the workplace posed issues quite as important for democracy—especially for the left—as did suffrage questions. To be sure, the growth of union bureaucracies and their increasing domination of union agendas did, very often, divert attention away from such matters—but they also regularly resurfaced, manifesting themselves not least in periodic contests between rank and file members and their officials.

This is not to say that Eley never mentions these matters. He observes the way trade unionism's mass basis made it an important factor in national life, and notes the rise in the strike statistics in the immediate pre-1914 period. As he remarks—though it will play less part in his overall narrative—the 1905 Revolution in Russia inextricably linked questions of work and democracy, wages and citizenship. And he does record both the costs of top-heavy centralism in labour movements, and also the way that it in turn became a big spur to unofficial militancy. He also remarks that the conundrum of 'reconciling the case for centralism with the demands of internal democracy and grassroots militancy...would become the source of enormous internal conflict'. They would, as he remarks, underpin 'rival visions of socialism'.[11]

What Eley suggests is that, in the consolidated organisation of social democratic parties and unions, something got lost along the way—in particular, the valuable aspects of the legacy of the utopian socialists of the earlier 19th century. The utopians (Saint-Simon, Fourier, Owen, Cabet and others) did, in practice, retreat into apolitical and often outlandish forms of experimental community building; often they were silent on how a real transition to a new society might be achieved; and they tended to be indifferent to political economy and the structural origins of class-based inequality. Social democrats after the 1860s explicitly repudiated the utopians here. However, there were other sides to the utopian legacy. One was the focus on producer co-operatives and 'social workshops', tied to a vision of self government. That part of the utopian legacy did not, I suggest, so much disappear as transmute and reappear on an immensely larger scale, no longer attached to experimental communities but as part of the 20th century repertoire of revolutionary workers' movements—most notably in the workers' councils and soviets.

What Eley, however, especially laments is the loss of the 'radical politics of gender' that characterised the early utopians: the critiques of marriage and of the family, of patriarchal relations between men and women, of the absence of mutuality and equality between the sexes. The second half of the 19th century witnessed a double movement, in which working class organisations came to accept the given basis of the wage relation and to organise and bargain collectively within this—learning the rules of the market game, as Hobsbawm expressed it—and at the same time tried to construct a form of family life fitted to this reality.[12] Its ideal assumption was a worker-husband who left every morning to earn a family wage while the wife remained behind doing household tasks and bringing up the children. Outside the skilled and better paid layers, this was often no more than a dream, for most working class wives continued to earn money when and how they could. This pattern of adjustment to the pressures of working class life in capitalist society had the effect of remaking the 'traditional' dependence of women on men. In the process, as Eley puts it:

> ...commitment to gender equality was lost. Visions of sexual freedom and alternatives to the patriarchal family were pushed to the dissident edges of the labour movements. Women were no longer addressed by means of an independent feminist platform but were treated either as mothers or potential workers. The early belief in sexual equality ('women's petty interests of the moment', as the German social democrat Clara Zetkin put it) became swallowed into the class struggle. Or, as Eleanor Marx exhorted in 1892, 'We will organise not as "women" but as *proletarians*...for us there is nothing but the working class movement'.[13]

In Eley's account, 'By choosing certain strategies of community defence over others, working class radicals shaped an enduring ideology of domesticity, limiting effective citizenship to men'.[14] And, as part of that process, they constructed an image of the working class itself, centred on the figure of the *male* manual worker:

> Across industrialising Europe, the ideal of the household managed by the non-working wife was available only to a minority. Women's earning power may have been vital to working families, but its status was practically and explicitly devalued. Thus in building the collective ideal of the working class—in shaping the disorderly facts of industrialisation into a basis for politics—socialists embraced only some parts of working class life while derogating others. In the centring of class identity, some working class experiences became valorised,

others ignored or effaced… Labour movements institutionalised precisely the systems of distinction that were least conducive to a genuinely inclusive and gender-blind working class political presence. While invoking the interests, authority, and collective agency of the working class as a whole, those movements were actually far more narrow and exclusionary.[15]

The world of the skilled trade unionist did not encompass the 'authentic' working class, any more than did that of the unskilled and unorganised labourers of pre-1914 Europe. What the left needed to do was to devise a politics for both, and to organise:

on two fronts of social dispossession: the working men's experience of long weary walks to work, exhausting labour, occupational injuries and diseases and grim periods of unemployment; and the lives of their wives at their own paid jobs, in local markets, dealing with landlords, charities and state institutions. The term 'labour movements' often implicitly suggested that the former was their province.

In Eley's reading, not until the 1960s would any proper recovery of the utopian legacy with respect to gender occur. He ties that recovery to the flowering of a new feminism.

It is undeniable that there is *some* truth in the story Eley tells. But he rather skates over the complexities, in offering an account in which 'the woman question' was always subordinated and even ignored in the pursuit of a 'class politics' that was resolutely masculinist. Socialism itself, he suggests, became—both in its vision and in the instruments shaped to fight for it—a one-sided male affair. There is a peculiar forgetfulness in Eley's story in a couple of respects. First, he never even mentions Engels and his *Origin of the Family, Private Property and the State*, a short book that maintained a fairly constant left readership, and whose pages both include a striking critical image of the modern working class family as itself divided between a 'bourgeois' husband and a 'proletarian' wife, and which envisages a future in which sexual relations will be founded solely on mutual attraction and not material dependence. Eley does note, though only in passing, that August Bebel's *Women and Socialism* was a bestseller in the socialist movement. Second, his implied critique of both Clara Zetkin and Eleanor Marx quite hides from view that, just as the 'left' was a field of contesting voices, so too was 'feminism'. There was always a practical and theoretical argument between 'bourgeois feminism' and 'socialist feminism'.[16]

Eley's treatment of the question seems too one-sided. Yet he himself provides some of the materials to question it. He opens his discussion of the pre-1914 period with the story of Edith Lanchester, a Social Democratic Federation (SDF) member from Battersea, who in 1895 announced her intention of living with James Sullivan in a 'free love' union. Edith and James were opposed in principle to marriage as a social institution because it destroyed women's independence. Edith's father and brothers intervened, having her hauled off to an asylum with a certificate of insanity signed by a mental specialist, Dr George Fielding Blandford. A campaign in her support won a writ of *habeas corpus*. Two commissioners in lunacy found Edith to be 'of sound mind, if misguided' and eventually ordered her discharge.

The left at the time was divided over the 'Lanchester case'. Her own party, the SDF, defended her rights and condemned the kidnapping, but while nodding to the Marxist critique of marriage it argued for pragmatic observance of 'the world as it is' and disavowed individual 'anarchistic action or personal revolt'. The SDF wanted to dissociate itself from 'free love' doctrines, and was joined by the Independent Labour Party (ILP), whose leader, Keir Hardie, also worried about socialism's bad name: 'Enemies of socialism know that such an escapade as that meditated by Miss Lanchester tends to discredit it among all classes.' However, there were other voices, among them dissenting SDF members, who saw Edith Lanchester's stand as a blow against 'this dark age of hypocrisy and ignorance', while Robert Blatchford's independent socialist weekly, *The Clarion*, declared, 'Socialists believe that a woman has a perfect right to do what she likes with her own body...in defiance of priests, laws, customs and cant'.[17] Blatchford's view was perhaps more widely shared on the left than Eley will allow.

What more general sense should we make of this story? One obvious point is that the left was divided in respect of this case, as indeed it would continue to be over all manner of questions. That suggests that we need to understand 'the left', not as a homogeneous body of opinion and organisation, but rather as a field of argument. Within that field, a whole variety of voices appear, some seemingly echoing half-forgotten voices from the past (and suggesting, by the way, that earlier utopian ideas about gender were not entirely lost), others offering ideas and terms that would burst forth again in different conditions—how very modern, for example, Blatchford's *Clarion* sounds! All of this means that the very definition of 'the left' presents a practical-theoretical problem, whose contours are liable to alter in different conditions, and which sets up important strategic questions for socialists.

In this respect, Eley's account is sometimes unsatisfactory. On the politics of gender, he states, 'The more consistent the socialism, one might say, the more easily feminist demands were postponed to the socialist future, because a sternly materialist standpoint insisted that none of these questions could be tackled while capitalism perdured'.[18]

This is very questionable. What or who is to count as 'consistent socialism', and what is this 'materialist standpoint'? As Eley himself documents in the second part of his book, it was the Bolsheviks who, in the immediate aftermath of the October Revolution, carried through legislation embodying the most complete set of feminist demands available at their time, far in advance of anything in the rest of the world. But then the Bolsheviks' version of 'materialism' was very different from that which Eley attributes to the left. Bolshevik politics involved a rediscovery of the revolutionary ideas of Karl Marx, ideas founded on a version of materialism that Eley seems not to understand well. The issues are quite fundamental, for they concern the book's central themes: democracy, socialist transformation, and the nature of the left.

How is democracy, and social transformation generally, to be achieved? 'In practice,' writes Eley, 'democratic goals can only ever be pursued against the resistance of dominant social groups'.[19] Expanding democracy is not just a matter of goodwill and understanding, but of struggle against resistance. Here we have half of a Marxist argument, and an important half. But only half. Back in 1845-1846, in *The German Ideology*, Marx and Engels made a similar point, in support of the necessity of revolution, but added to it something deeper:

> Both for the production on a mass scale of this communist consciousness, and for the success of the cause itself, the alteration of men on a mass scale is necessary, an alteration which can only take place in a practical movement, a *revolution*; this revolution is necessary, therefore, not only because the *ruling* class cannot be overthrown in any other way, but also because

the class *overthrowing* it can only in a revolution succeed in ridding itself of all the muck of ages and become fitted to found society anew.[20]

Socialism is not just a matter of overcoming ruling class resistance. Those who do the overcoming must also transform themselves in that struggle. That whole argument rests on a *materialist* position spelled out by Marx in a brief but critical set of notes in the spring of 1845. Materialism up till then, he suggested, treated reality only as an object of contemplation, and not as 'sensuous human activity, practice, not subjectively'. It had been idealist philosophy which had developed—albeit abstractly—'the active side'. Against 'old materialism' Marx upheld a 'new materialism' which no longer treated human beings as the (passive) creatures of their circumstances, but insisted that they defined themselves through their own activity: 'The coincidence of the changing of circumstances and of human activity or self changing can be conceived and rationally understood only as *revolutionary practice*'.[21]

This is a 'sternly materialist standpoint', but one leading to conclusions very different from those Eley attributes to those (unnamed) socialist thinkers who said women must wait for socialism to liberate them. Whether the subject be women, or workers, Marx insists, they can only change their conditions insofar as they themselves are active and thus transform themselves. It is upon this foundation that Marx, in the 1860s, wrote the opening words of the Provisional Rules of the First International: 'The emancipation of the working classes must be conquered by the working classes themselves'.[22]

Such ideas will be familiar to many readers of this journal. They provide the basis for drawing a fundamental distinction within the ranks of those identifying themselves as 'the left' over the past century and a half. The point was made brilliantly by the late Hal Draper, who distinguished between 'two souls of socialism' that he termed 'socialism from above' and 'socialism from below'.[23] The essence of 'socialism from above' is the idea that some 'saviour from on high'—clever intellectuals, a party, an elected body of parliamentary MPs, etc—will carry out the emancipation of society on its behalf. Such a conception, Marx suggested in his third 'Thesis on Feuerbach', underlay all those varieties of 'materialism' which declared that men are the products of their circumstances and upbringing, forgetting that men change their circumstances and that the educator must himself be educated. If human beings are determined, rather than self determining, then changing society must be the activity of a group superior to society, which itself somehow escapes determination. The doctrine of 'socialism from above' is inherently elitist, indeed reproduces fundamental assumptions of class society. It denies the crucial role of popular creative development in history; it is, indeed, in the strictest sense 'counter-revolutionary.' By contrast, 'socialism from below' insists that society's transformation is necessarily the work of the majority, the product of their own self activity and self organisation. This doctrine is inherently revolutionary, as well as being inherently democratic. In general terms, we can view the whole history of socialism as an ongoing contest between adherents of these two opposed traditions.

That contest is central to the equally long-running argument between 'reform' and 'revolution'. This is not, unfortunately, how Eley understands that argument. For him, while democratic goals can only be pursued against the resistance of dominant social groups, the decisive political and philosophical question becomes something different: 'How far can attacks on the legitimacy of private interests stay compatible with the democratic principle, without requiring the use of force and the damaging of basic rights, while the new collectivist system is being installed?' Divisions over this question, he goes on to suggest, have been 'one of the main dividing lines between reformist and revolutionary movements'.[24] This reduces the argument to a debate between socialism and liberalism about the degree to which private interests can and should be overcome, and about whether force is a legitimate means to achieve this. What quite disappears is any conception of popular self organisation as the critical issue. Nor does any issue of principle appear to divide those who stand on either side.

Eley presents a Marx who seems something of a caricature. His Marx in 1848 was 'trapped in Blanquism's practical logic', despite his break with the conspiratorial traditions of existing revolutionary groups:

> ...moving ahead of popular consciousness, [Marx] still aimed to steer the masses towards insurrectionary showdown... Marx and his friends claimed to know the future by virtue of understanding history's inescapable progress. This put them in a superior relation to the masses, divining the true direction of their interests.[25]

In a footnote, he expands on this idea: 'When knowledge of a future outcome is claimed, a manipulative approach to popular politics easily follows, in which the masses are moved to the appropriate destination, whether or not they understand'.[26] In this manner, Eley gives flesh to an earlier argument, that the legacy of Blanquism continued in the shape of vanguardism, which he defines as 'the idea that minorities of disciplined revolutionaries, equipped with sophisticated theories and superior virtue, could anticipate the direction of popular hopes, act decisively in their name, and in the process radicalise the masses'. This is the politics he attributes to Marx—in flat contradiction to the historical record.

What did Marx actually argue during and after the 1848 revolutions? Practical experience in 1848 showed, he suggested, that bourgeois forces rapidly lose their appetite for revolution in the face of working class revolutionary activity, and come to play a reactionary role. What is the status of this argument? It is, surely, that we can learn something about who can and can't be expected to be consistent and trustworthy allies in a revolutionary crisis. It suggests, moreover, that workers need to *understand* this reality, so that they will not be misled by false friends. How is this 'manipulative'? Does it involve any element of acting in the masses' name under the illusion that such action will radicalise them? Not at all. What it does involve is openly expressing a standpoint. Marx and Engels, like their successors, disdained to hide their views. The test of their ideas would lie, in part, in the clarity with which they expressed them, the means they developed to promulgate them, and, above all, the degree to which they were actually recognised by real workers' movements as summarising their actual experience and showing a road forward. There is nothing Blanquist, or manipulative, in any of this—unless one supposes, as Marx decidedly did not, that workers couldn't think for themselves.

Eley is not even very consistent in his account of Marx. He notes in passing that the period after Marx's death, when labour movements bifurcated into 'political' and 'industrial' wings, each pursuing its own reformist ends, undermined Marx's vision of a unified emancipatory struggle and that, in that process, Marx's own commitment to 'direct participatory democracy' (exemplified in his comments on the Paris Commune of 1871) was also lost, as the battle for democracy was, for a period, reduced almost entirely to parliamentary forms.[27] Now, we can either have a Marx whose thought was hopelessly split between 'Blanquist manipulation' and a belief in 'direct participatory democracy', as Eley seems to imply, or we can have a more consistent Marx—much truer to the historical record—who completely rejected Blanquism and all other forms of 'socialism from above', and whose thinking was always that of a revolutionary and democratic socialism 'from below'.

What is true is that Marx's revolutionary ideas were significantly changed by the generation of socialist intellectuals who came to leadership in the social democratic parties after Marx and Engels quit the scene. In the hands of thinkers like Kautsky and Hilferding, the revolutionary ideas of Marx were reduced to a 'scientism', in which 'historical laws' were somehow supposed to guarantee socialist advance, independently of what actual historical men and women actually did and thought.

The development of mass social democratic parties, committed to parliamentary methods and attached to national unions, with their own bureaucracies, would pose new problems of theory, strategy and tactics to the left. These developments provided the setting for the Europe-wide debates, in the two decades before 1914, about 'revisionism' and 'economism'—the first form in which divisions between 'left' and 'right' manifested themselves with some degree of clarity. What gradually became apparent was that the very institutions and practices of European labour movements were becoming, even as they were being created and developed, not only means but also impediments to democratic and socialist advance. This growing awareness is signalled, for example, in Rosa Luxemburg's writings. In 1899, sharply rebutting Eduard Bernstein in her *Social Reform and Revolution*, she attributed the influence of 'revisionism' to the continuing weight of the 'petty bourgeoisie' within social democracy. Seven years later, when she wrote *The Mass Strike*, her whole emphasis had shifted: now she saw the very structures of existing social democracy in Germany, with its divisions into parliamentarist and trade union wings, as itself the source of the problem. Now it appeared that the barriers the working class must surmount if it was to overthrow capitalism included not only the combined forces of capital and the state, but also the very organisations it had itself created in pursuit of its aims. Now the left must also take account of the conservatism of the party and trade union bureaucracies, and their readiness to hold back working class insurgency.

That discovery—variously nuanced in the different countries where industrial capitalism was most developed—necessarily had momentous consequences for socialist theory, for strategy and tactics.[28] How, in the first place, should the emergence of these 'revisionist' tendencies be explained—as the product of a thin layer of relatively privileged officials and 'labour aristocrats', or as the outcome of deeper contradictory processes of working class incorporation within the routines of modern capitalism? Second, how far would their conservative impulses carry the leaders of the parties and the unions towards accommodation with the ruling order? Would they merely seek to blur the contradictions between capital and labour, or actually change sides? Third, what kinds of activity did these new realities imply for those who held fast to the idea of working class self emancipation? How far and in what form should the left break organisationally with organised reformist bodies? Was it sufficient to debate fundamental questions within the framework of existing organisations? Should socialists rely on the emergence of spontaneous rank and file opposition to union and party bureaucracies? Should they organise entirely separately and in complete isolation from the reformist bodies, whether in new specifically revolutionary parties or in newly founded militant unions? How should revolutionaries relate to the large masses of workers who remained under the sway of the conservative bureaucracies within the official labour movements? Here was a mass of complex questions, whose solution would require both a rediscovery and remaking of Marxism's core meaning in the light of new conditions, as well as the practical testing of different solutions.

Nor did these problems arise in isolation. By the start of the 20th century the European powers had largely divided the globe between them in a set of competing empires and spheres of influence. Great Power rivalries were building up, military budgets were rising, nationalist sentiments were being promoted (along with support for anti-foreigner feeling and racism towards colonial subjects), and questions about the rights of the nations in Europe's ramshackle absolutist empires were being posed with growing sharpness. Across most of Europe, there were still millions of small farmers whose political allegiances were in doubt: what policy should working class parties adopt to them and their concerns—or should they effectively ignore them and focus only on farm labourers on big estates, as Kautsky urged?

Solutions to these and other dilemmas were not quickly and immediately available. It would take the immense crisis produced by the First World War and its aftermath for anything like clear answers to emerge.

Geoff Eley is a good historian, in the sense that he does report the various issues and debates, often with a wealth of fascinating detail. He recognises the emerging conflict within unions between the growing bureaucracies and 'the elemental democracies of the shop floor'. He records how the SPD and other social democratic parties hankered after bourgeois respectability, the parliamentarist nature of the parties, their disinterest in (indeed in Kautsky's case, their direct opposition to) aspirations to workers' control in industry, their inattention to colonialism and to feminist issues, and so on. But he reaches a limit. At no point does he 'take sides', in the sense of arguing where the logic of any position might lead, even though he clearly feels that many of these positions were mistaken or problematical. Nor, therefore, does he press hard at that difficult but vital question, who or what is to count as 'the left'? Was 'the left' a potentially united entity, or did deep inherent divisions mean that its major wings were bound to come into sharp conflict? Such questions haunt the rest of his story.

1914-1923

The ten years from 1914 to 1923 represented a critical period in the development of the left in Europe, and indeed across the world. The unprecedented mass killing and deprivations of the First World War occasioned an immense wave of popular radicalisation. Already developing contradictions in emerging labour organisations came to a head. Working class and socialist organisations were riven with bitter conflicts and splits: between union and party bureaucracies on one hand and the aspirations and demands of rank and file workers on the other; between the defenders of parliamentarism and moderation and newly self conscious proponents of revolutionary politics; between different conceptions of the nature of socialism and equally of Marxism. New, if temporary, alliances were formed, for example between revolutionary Marxists and anarcho-syndicalists.

This period threw up fundamental problems which would continue to be central to socialist argument for the next 80 years. Because they were not resolved adequately—ie practically—the appalling slaughter of the First World War was followed only two decades later by six more years of even more terrible death and destruction, in what Eric Hobsbawm dubbed the Thirty Years War of the 20th century.

Before 1914, famously, the Second International passed apparently united resolutions declaring its militant opposition to impending war. In

August 1914, however, all but the Russian and Bulgarian socialist parties fell in behind their respective national governments, contributing to the pro-war hysteria that marked its outbreak. In country after country the socialist opponents of imperialist war found themselves in isolated minorities. As Eley records, for right wing socialist party leaders and union bureaucrats, the war brought a kind of 'socialism': they were courted and integrated into government, in return for their abandoning the practice of class opposition. It meant, for the working class, as well as mass conscription and rising death rates at the front, speed-up in the factories, the suspension of factory regulations, lower safety standards, the freezing of basic union rights and falling living standards: 'Thus the socialists' integration into government was matched by rank and file alienation'.[29]

Given the disorientation imposed by official social democracy, the speed and degree with which organised popular discontent manifested itself was impressive. Strikes—at first over 'economic' and soon over 'political' issues—became ever more frequent as the war progressed. Militant workers created new organisational forms like the Internal Commissions in Italy or the Clyde Workers' Committee and shop stewards movement in Britain. The stage was set for deep splits and regroupments in existing left organisations. Internationally, the left managed to organise two small anti-war conferences in Switzerland. In Germany the SPD expelled its left wing in 1917, producing a new Independent Party, the USPD. However, as Eley notes, the new party 'lacked either a coherent vision or a solid popular organisation'.[30] The same was true of other broad left oppositions such as developed in France, in the Italian 'Maximalists' or the Leeds anti-war convention in Britain. The strongest expression of militancy, economic or political, came at rank and file level.

In the latter part of the war and after, the old European order was to be shaken to its core by popular militancy. The critical question became: what will follow? Who will master the popular explosions, and where will Europe (and the world) go? No serious practical answer could be given to that unless, simultaneously, the question of defining 'the left' was also posed clearly. If the 1914–1918 war had already brought that issue sharply to the fore, the revolutionary wave from 1917 made it still more urgent.

The same essential elements that would soon convulse the whole of Europe were, as Eley remarks, central to the first revolution, in Russia in February 1917. That revolution drew on the militancy of women from the textile mills and the bread lines, a huge wave of strikes and the mutinying of troops. In the very process of the uprising, workers and soldiers recreated the institutions they had first invented in 1905, the soviets (popular councils). February thus produced a situation in Russia of 'dual power' in which rival institutions—on one side a provisional government, on the other the soviet—contested for practical power. However, those who initially came to head the soviet were the 'moderate left' who fell back into the position of the social democratic right across Europe: they resisted popular demands for change and reform, defended the polices of the Provisional Government, and continued to support the war. The Menshevik view, summed up by the German socialist Karl Kautsky as 'masterly limitation', was, Eley suggests, 'principled and realistic as an assessment of Russia's existing developmental resources'. However, as he goes on to point out, 'this strategy remained doctrinaire, abysmally unsuited for the popular mobilisation of 1917... Mensheviks found themselves constantly trying to hold popular hopes back, within the bourgeois revolution's normative limits... [Their policy] trapped the Mensheviks into a debilitating logic of incorporation... They continued substituting for the social force—the liberal bourgeoisie—they believed the rightful bearer of the revolution'.[31] Time and again both the Mensheviks and the Social Revolutionaries resisted popular demands for an end to the war, for a solution to peasant land hunger and a resolution of the social struggle over wages, prices and the control of industry—demands emerging from a still radicalising population.

Such inner conflicts—between newly promoted governments and radical popular movements, where proponents of so called 'moderate' policies sought to demobilise the very forces that had propelled them into office—would characterise every significant subsequent revolution. Time and again such conflicts would derail those revolutions.[32]

What made the Russian Revolution unusual was the presence of Lenin's Bolshevik Party. During 1917 'pressure for resolving dual power in favour of the soviet reached a crescendo'—and only the Bolsheviks consistently urged that resolution.[33] Eley sums the matter up well: 'Bolshevism rose to power by organising this popular radicalisation'.[34] As he also shows, Bolshevism in reality was far from the widespread caricature of a disciplined vanguard party. Additionally, only Lenin's Bolsheviks had a practical pro-peasant policy: 'The worst failure of the non-Bolshevik left' (the

Mensheviks and SRs) was their refusal to back peasant demands, and actions, for immediate land reform. In 1917, the Bolsheviks 'alone took the peasants seriously'.[35]

Eley's account of 1917 in Russia is refreshing after the mountains of reactionary nonsense so many historians have served up. Unlike other historians, he gives proper weight to the internationalist perspective that underlay the theory of 'permanent revolution'. I would only question his account in two respects. First, he doesn't discuss what might have happened had the Menshevik policy succeeded. Had power not passed to the soviets, the revolution's popular base in the working class, the army and the countryside would have been demobilised. Menshevik success would have opened space for the victory, not of liberal moderation, but of the far right, represented by both the military high command (in a more successful re-run of the Kornilov coup attempt) and the Russian employers.[36] The war, with its immense loss of life, would have dragged on; fierce and bloody repression of workers, peasants and mutinous soldiers would have been instituted. 'Dual power' could not last: resolving it against the soviet would have stripped the popular revolution of its gains. Second, while Eley finds Lenin's 'powerful unity of conviction and action' admirable, he finds 'less appealing' Lenin's 'belief in splitting—his drive for polemical clarification, brutally distancing his rivals'.[37] But a 'nicer' Lenin would have compromised with the Mensheviks, not challenged the Second International's betrayals, and let the revolution go hang. It was precisely the sharpness of Lenin's political intellect, his willingness to follow a correct idea to its conclusions, indeed a readiness to split when necessary, that made him effective. Eley's term 'rivals' diminishes the problem, as if the matter were one of competition among potential partners. Those whom Lenin 'distanced' were political opponents, whether parties or individuals, whose influence would, if unchallenged, have the effect of undermining or reversing the revolutionary struggle.

After the Russian Revolution, the question posed was, as Eley rightly asks, was there a possibility that revolutionary socialism could also triumph elsewhere in Europe? Here Eley expresses doubts:

> Russian extremes created chances for the left that weren't available elsewhere in Europe. Some wartime circumstances were generic—notably, the labour movement's incorporation via patriotism, bringing gains for leaders but

hardship for the rank and file. But in other ways, Russian circumstances were least like the others, because the thinness of civil society left Russia exceptionally vulnerable to generalised breakdown, which the West's more developed institutional resources forestalled.[38]

The theme is 'Gramscian', with a Eurocommunist inflexion.[39] But the analysis is weak. In what exactly did the 'thinness of civil society' in Russia consist, by comparison with Western Europe, and especially as far as strategy was concerned? The crucial 'more developed institutional resources' in the West were those of organised reformism, notably as they were embodied in the social democratic parties and union bureaucracies. There is no question that overcoming their conservatism would be a central strategic question for revolutionary socialists, but a question that required, let us emphasise, an answer cast in terms of *politics* and not of sociological determinism.

Eley's account seems muddled. He notes how the Russian Revolution caught the imagination of socialists across Europe, cracking apart Kautsky's and Hilferding's tired old version of Marxism as a theory of historical inevitability. Now human creative agency could again be given its proper, central place. But Eley argues that the revolutionary politics of the new generation suffered in two respects. On one hand, 'post-revolutionary constitutions were still conceived in parliamentary terms,' while on the other, 'the new revolutionaries neglected building the coalitions so crucial to the practical survival of revolutionary regimes, given the social, religious and ethnic heterogeneity of all European countries.' The first criticism ignores the way the socialist movement divided sharply over whether 'post-revolutionary constitutions' should be conceived in parliamentary terms, and thus how these divisions set up new strategic and tactical questions. As for the second, the issue of coalitions was certainly crucial. However, it was not merely about the survival of revolutionary regimes, but about whether revolution ought to happen at all. Furthermore, the problem of 'coalitions' was not just about sociological heterogeneity within Europe, but above all concerned the question of how to respond to the existence of varied political currents within the working class itself.

What is striking about the years 1918–1923 is the combination of immensely powerful popular revolutionary impulses with an absence of strategic clarity among the newly emerging revolutionary socialist parties and groups. Eley catches something of this with the remark that (in Germany) 'during 1919-1921, the passions and hopes of rank and file insurgents constantly outstripped the capacity of existing left organisations to represent them',[40] a judgment which could be extended well beyond Germany. If one thing tended to unite the emerging revolutionary left, it was a rejection of parliamentarism and an aspiration to a form of society based on workers' councils, an impulse that took on different organisational forms and names in different countries. However, the realisation of such visions necessarily required a strategic capacity that was mostly wanting. For 'council communism', Eley's term for these impulses, brought the movement into direct conflict with trade union officialdom and with the leadership of the social democratic parties. In order to win out, its supporters must necessarily face up to a range of practical as well as theoretical issues. Eley mentions some of these—although his list is curiously ordered:

> There were huge areas council communists ignored. Questions of women, the family, and the sexual division of labour were one. Coalition building was another, for the council movement refused to worry about peasants, petty bourgeoisie and other non-proletarian social groups. Council militants were untroubled by the administrative consequences of organising revolutionary government around the point of production. If the councils had a factory rather than a territorial basis, training workers for running production rather than society in general, then how would the non-economic functions of government be addressed? How would the councils deal with social welfare and education? How successfully could they represent the interests of non-workers?[41]

Yet if these weaknesses were real—and they were—even more central was the question, how are the defenders of such revolutionary programmes to win over real, practical majorities, given the still predominant influence of social democracy and its associated union bureaucracies within popular movements? Council communism's opponents were not simply the capitalist classes and the state machineries, but the forces of 'moderation' inside the labour movements of Europe. 'The left' was now not just openly divided—it was facing in opposite directions.

Nowhere was this more apparent than in Germany. November 1918 saw the Kaiser's regime fall, in a rerun—on a still more massive scale—of

February 1917 in Russia. Also as in Russia, an immediate division appeared between 'moderates' and 'militants.' The SPD, which had supported the war until the end, was suddenly thrust into government, alongside a left whose forces lacked anything like the ideological clarity the Bolsheviks had possessed and won in Russia. Eley comments on the SPD, 'The most striking thing about the German revolution was the unrelenting intransigence of the SPD's moderation. Rather than harnessing working class militancy, the leaders did their best to suppress it'.[42] Even the term 'moderation' is understated: the SPD leaders allied themselves with the former Kaiser's army high command, and deliberately assisted in the creation of the *Freikorps*, a right wing military formation established to destroy working class militancy. While the SPD were hard-headed and determined, the USPD offered no convincing alternative, despite attracting large new forces, while the newly formed Spartacists and the rest of the far left were fragmented and inexperienced. Indeed, within weeks of their founding conference, the Spartacists allowed themselves to be drawn into a minority effort at socialist revolution, the Spartacist uprising of January 1919, which was put down with ferocity. Among those deliberately killed were the new party's leaders, Rosa Luxemburg and Karl Liebknecht. Urged on by the SPD leaders, the *Freikorps* marched about Germany crushing working class resistance with murderous force.

In Eley's account, the emergent workers' councils in Germany represented the possibility of a 'third way' between the SPD's constitutionalism and the insurrectionary politics of the left, inspired by the Bolshevik Revolution.[43] For Eley, the tragedy is that the SPD failed to offer any support to such a 'third way'. He finds Ebert and the other SPD leaders 'lamentably unimaginative in failing to harness this popular upsurge… [The SPD's] constitutionalist course was imposed at a double cost: the bases of authoritarianism in the state and economy had been saved, indeed renewed, in their time of greatest vulnerability; and the best expressions of popular democracy had been rebuffed, even brutally repressed'.[44] He continues:

> The real tragedy of 1918-1919 was not the failure to force through a socialist revolution. The abstract merits of such a course may be endlessly debated, but it could only have succeeded through a long and bloody civil war, and for many socialists this was too high a price to pay. The real tragedy was the SPD's excessively legalistic, stolidly unimaginative, and wholly conservative

notion of what a democratically ordered polity might be. In 1918, the SPD had an unprecedented chance to expand the frontiers of democracy, both by dismantling the bases of authoritarianism in the discredited *ancien régime* and by harnessing the new popular energies the council movement released. The chances of a further-reaching reformism were squandered. It was by its own democratic lights that the SPD failed the test.[45]

Here his judgment seems to me to be seriously at fault. It is not that socialist revolution could be on the immediate agenda in 1918 or early 1919. That would require the left winning a majority among German workers and others in support of such a project. 'Civil war' was, in any case, unavoidable: it is exactly what occurred in Germany, on and off, from 1919 to 1923. The real problem with Eley is that he thinks it appropriate to chide the SPD leaders for their policies and lack of imagination, as if they could in any sense still be counted as part of the left. It was the achievement of the Zimmerwald left during the war to realise that the SPD and the other parties of the Second International had already not only declared their bankruptcy as agencies of socialist change, but become part of the problem rather than of the solution. The fact that the SPD still gained the largest slice of the working class vote was, strategically, of no more significance than the adhesion of many workers in Britain to the Tory and Liberal parties. The real tragedy in Germany was the left's failure to find a way to challenge and transcend the SPD's hold over workers' political loyalties, a hold that was—as Eley notes—never a given. Separate communist organisation did not even appear until after the November Revolution. The Spartacists, and subsequently the KPD, were marked by lack of clarity about how to respond to the explosion of popular movements, and subsequently veered between ultra-leftism and rightist accommodation in ways that cost the German left dearly—and, in costing them dearly, it would cost a lot more, not just for German working people but for the whole world.[46]

The struggle to gain such clarity was hard. An entire theoretical and organisational heritage had to be critically explored and remade, often in the heat of difficult new developments. Nor was the problem in any sense confined to Germany. In Italy, for example, the central source of confusion lay in the PSI (the Socialist Party of Italy), whose leader, Serrati, was responsible for the infamous statement, 'We, as Marxists, interpret history; we do not make it.' Eley comments:

Maximalist failings were an object lesson in how not to conduct a revolution. They fed expectations without resolving them. They fanned a mood of revolutionary excitement but refused to shape it into a revolutionary challenge. They fashioned socialism into a barrier against the bourgeois world and from behind this ideological stockade released a fusillade of rhetorical provocation. But when the masses took them at their word and acted, they counselled discipline and patience.[47]

He goes on to add, rather confusingly for those who have just read him on Germany, that:

One lesson of Maximalist failings, then, was organisational: the need for revolutionary leadership, a Bolshevik party. This was Bordiga's position, and during 1920 Gramsci joined him... Italian socialism encapsulated the left's dilemma in the post-war revolutionary conjuncture. The obstacles to socialist revolution, in Italy no less than Germany, were formidable. But among them was a failure of revolutionary leadership, which 'faded away at the moment of truth'.[48]

It might seem, then, that Eley agrees that the problem in Germany too was the failure of revolutionary leadership. And might we then expect some discussion of the specific failures of both the German and Italian communists, and of what a 'Bolshevik leadership' ought actually to have done in the midst of the crises that convulsed these countries?

Not at all. Eley's real agenda is different. He is interested in asking how the 'transition to a new social democratic era' might have been achieved, even if that might then become the prelude to 'a restabilisation of capitalism'.[49] After their electoral successes in November 1919, and again at the height of the factory occupations in September 1920, Eley thinks the PSI's best hope was to join and help shape 'a broader democratic bloc'.[50]

In both Germany and Italy, Eley looks for what never had a basis: 'A successful non-Bolshevik left needed the best of both worlds: radical yet democratic extraparliamentary energies mobilised and channelled through the parliamentary process'.[51] There is no sense of the process, repeated time and again in potentially revolutionary situations in the course of the 20th century, whereby just such 'channelling through the parliamentary process' is the very means by which extraparliamentary popular energies have been regularly *demobilised*. Nor is any concrete analysis offered of the emerging shapes of the actual 'radical and extraparliamentary energies' that most certainly did develop.

Within a remarkably short space of time after the 1920 factory occupations, Mussolini's fascists had taken power. It was a stunning defeat for the left, and indeed for democracy in any sense.[52] But, extraordinarily, Eley has nothing to say about it, about how it happened, whether it was preventable, and what it can tell us about the left's failings. The lapse in his narrative is astonishing—and he is, as we'll see, to repeat it on an even more serious scale in his next section.

Part of the difficulty with Eley's account of the whole period consists in an apparent failure to understand what, in shorthand, we might term 'Leninism'. While he gives a generally good account of the Russian Revolution itself, his sense of the logic of Lenin's politics is deficient. He writes that, once insurrection in Europe was no longer on the agenda, 'Lenin would find himself, willy–nilly, conceding the importance of parliamentary, trade union and other "legal" fields of action, however tactical, subordinate, or cynical these concessions claimed to be'.[53] Lenin's whole political career before 1917 is thus dismissed: his arguments for and involvement in factory and union agitation, the Bolsheviks' work in the Duma, their activity in 'sickness funds' and so on.[54] Eley makes nothing of Lenin's reproof to European 'left' communists in *Left Wing Communism: An Infantile Disorder*. And he makes nothing, either, of the whole debate within the new Communist International about the importance of 'united fronts'. He does note that the new Communist Parties faced national 'lefts' that included a whole gamut of positions from left reformists to ultra-lefts, identifying this as their 'thorniest dilemma: how successfully they shaped such militancy would decisively influence the *kind* of Communist parties they would become'.[55] But what the parameters of debate among them were, and which were the better and the worse responses, he doesn't say. Nor, therefore, does Eley generally explain why various revolutionary attempts in this period were defeated. Were they simply inappropriate leftist adventures, were they overcome by the 'thickness' of civil society's institutions in West European countries, or did serious failings in communist strategy and tactics play any significant role? Eley is generally not very interested in the revolutionary left, especially as far as its actual politics are concerned, and thus there are no direct answers to such questions in his book. Sometimes, as in his brief remarks on the failed Hungarian soviet revolution of 1919, it seems as if these things just happened—rather like his treatment of Mussolini's victory in Italy.

In part because he treats these matters as relatively unimportant, Eley's judgment on the political outcome of the period has two faces. On one side, he sees the split within international socialism—most obviously represented by the sharp division between social democrat and communist, between the Second and Third Internationals—as 'disfiguring the left's politics until the flux of 1956-1968 and beyond'.[56] On the other, he sees the years of war and revolution as bringing real gains for democracy and for the left: 1918 brought them to the brink of governing for the first time; they benefited from universal suffrage, emerging social rights, a large increment of reform. Those gains were sustained by extraparliamentary social movements, ranging from the huge growth in trade unions to women's movements of various kinds along with a wide array of single-issue campaigns, many of them locally based. 'Indeed, the failures of central European socialists to break through to socialism during the revolutions of 1918-1919 mattered far less than the new democratic capacities and legal resources that the improved constitutional frameworks now supplied'.[57]

Was the split in the left at the time disfiguring, or necessary? What could a 'unity' resting on the suppression of profound differences have achieved? How could the followers of the murdered Rosa Luxemburg sit in the same organisation with those who organised her killing? What really 'disfigured' the politics of the left was not the split, but the trajectories of the two sides thereafter. As for the social and political gains of the period, it seems reasonable to ask how securely founded they were. In this respect, the debacles in Italy and Hungary were as much indicators of crises that would, all too soon, convulse democracy and the left alike.

There are fundamental issues here. To approach them, we must step back from Eley's text, to explore the rational core of the 'Leninism' that Eley opposes and misunderstands, indeed to argue, in Lukács's words, that 'the organisation and tactics of Bolshevism are the only possible consequence of Marxism'.[58]

Marxism's political project is the self emancipation of the working class, as the key to the emancipation of humanity. That requires the self constitution of the working class as a collective subject aiming to abolish its own condition of wage slavery. This is, it must be stressed, a political project, and not some inevitable outcome inscribed in imagined laws of history. 'Barbarism'—its potential shapes in advanced capitalism including fascism, nuclear warfare and ecological degradation—always remains as an alternative. History always poses choices.

The key to the Marxist revolutionary project is working class agency, consciousness and organisation. Its crucial opponent is ruling class ideology, itself arising not simply from the obvious effects of capitalist media and the like, but also from the everyday workings of capitalist economy and politics. Working people, divided among themselves in manifold ways by competition, come to see their alienated existence within capitalist social relations as 'natural', even if they contest aspects of this alienation. Popular consciousness, in Gramsci's phrase, is inherently 'contradictory', containing in spontaneous combination elements of the most advanced and backward thought and activity. Yet it is this working class, with its actual contradictory tendencies of self development, which Marxism envisions as the salvation of humanity.

The realities of life within the exploitative and oppressive social relations of capitalist society constantly regenerate forms of opposition to the status quo. That opposition takes practical appearance in an enormous variety of shapes, in a multiform array of 'social movements'. Never and nowhere are such movements, especially as they take on mass form, composed either of members only of a single class, or of all the members of any one class. Rather, constructed out of diverse social networks, they typically contain within themselves a wide spectrum of opinions, aspirations and prejudices. Just as the working class as a political actor is anything but homogeneous in its outlook, so it is with the movements in which it (variably) participates. 'Consciousness'—theoretical and practical alike—develops unevenly, at different speeds and degrees and in divergent directions.

Movements are themselves networks of social relations and activity marked by inner contestation and practical argument. They are not characterised by unified and coherent ideologies. Furthermore, they are anything but immune to influence by their opponents, or by ruling class ideas. What the debates within movements concern is not just general ideas, or goals, but also the very meaning and nature of the movements themselves, the kinds of practical methods it is appropriate for them to employ, the ways they ought to organise themselves, particular strategies and tactics and so forth. Movement opponents—notably employers and states—have a decided interest in these various debates. Where, as in liberal democracies, they have learned that they cannot easily exist without movement-based oppositions, they have definite interests in shaping the forms such movements take.

What they prefer are movements without teeth, led by 'responsible' people who use their leadership positions to contain supporters within the 'normal channels' of legality and constitutional respectability, and to oppose and demobilise more radical currents. They want unions that do not step beyond wage demands to challenge 'managerial prerogatives', just as in the 19th century they wanted even Friendly Societies to remain within the bounds of decency and good order.[59] And ruling classes have various factors working for them in their search for self limiting movements: not only the everyday effects of the very workings of capitalism itself, in which the wages system and employer authority come to seem 'natural', but also the mechanisms of law, media influence, and even the material and symbolic rewards offered to co-optable and 'statesmanlike' leaders.

However, contrary to those theories of ideology which see nothing but ruling class domination, the actual experiences of exploitation and oppression within capitalist society produce countervailing pressures. There are dual tendencies, both to the containment and to the regeneration of opposition. As a result, the interior life of movements consists of permanent contestation of ideas—permanent ideological struggle, not least 'over the terms in which the actors in the class struggle are to construe their experience of it'. The very institutions and practices of movements are generated in a history of victories, defeats and compromises which mark working class experience, and through which both ruling class ideology and popular experience come in part to constitute each other mutually.[60] Marxists are numbered among the participants in the arguments within and about what movements are, can be, and should do and say.

These struggles have to be grasped theoretically, not just in abstract and general terms, but in relation to a succession of concrete and particular situations, which are always changing. A Marxism, on the one hand, which does not deal with the concrete and immediate is condemned to practical irrelevance, to mere academicism. On the other hand, a set of oppositional ideas that does not constantly seek to tease out the dialectical interrelations between concrete and abstract, between the particular moment and the totality, is open to 'economism' and other forms of partial critique. Thus, for example, it can ignore the varieties of forms of oppression (and resistance to oppression) that constitute the whole concrete situation. Each specific situation poses strategic and tactical issues for all sides, in which the various forces at play may learn, devise new stratagems, respond and invent. Movement opponents may put forward new means by which they may seek to confine or disrupt movement activity, in ways whose implications are not always easily decoded. Movements in this sense are always, in Shandro's term, 'in the strategic sights' of their adversaries, compelling ideological struggle *within* movements over the interpretation of events along with the meanings and purposes of opponents' actions and words.[61] Such conflicts concern battles not just over matters of 'distribution' or 'rights', but over movements' very self constitution, organisation and self understanding.

Each situation thus constitutes a significant event, whose outcome will have consequences for future struggles. Every separate event is always relatively 'open', its outcome depending on who does and says what. All large and small events in the class struggle have 'turning points', moments when the practical and ideological stances adopted by the various parties and the actions they undertake set the stage for what is possible next. If this is most obvious in the case of 'revolutionary situations', the principle is by no means restricted to these. Events involve narratives of struggle, involving consciousness, organisation and the reformulation of ideas in the light of experience. Marxists, to be effective, have to be able to respond creatively to the concrete developments occurring within each particular situation.

In all of this, the revolutionary socialist standpoint remains that outlined in the *Communist Manifesto*: stressing the basic incompatibility of interests that lies at the heart of capitalism, advancing arguments for the maximum unity of the movement, always holding to the overall socialist goal of working class power. What is quite alien to this is the kind of narrow 'classism' that Eley imputes to the left, in which the focus necessarily falls on apparently immediate working class interests. Here one of Lenin's central arguments in his much-maligned early pamphlet *What Is To Be Done?* is vital: socialists have to advance the interests of *all the oppressed*, acting always as 'tribunes of the people'. Working class power as a goal requires that Marxists struggle to advance the interests of all those who are oppressed in different ways within class society, and must fight for those interests within working class movements themselves. Marxism, in other words, always involves a *critical* stance towards the very working class movements that it seeks to influence and advance.[62] The vital interest of the working class is to constitute itself as the hegemonic force within all movements, whether against national, gender, racist or any other form of oppression, since the alternative is always its own division, its own narrowness of outlook and aspiration—and thus its own containment within capitalist limits.

In this light, Marxism must be a developing rather than a fixed and finished theory, advancing itself through continual interrogation of movement practice and ideas, and in a permanent dialogue between Marxist organisations and the movements in which they participate and intervene. Its proponents cannot simply be 'educators', for they have to be constantly open to learning. The impulses to Marxism's own creative development often come, not from 'within' organised Marxist parties and groups, but from 'without', from the inventive practice of movements themselves.[63] Indeed, one important criterion by which to judge Marxists themselves consists in their capacity to listen and learn as well as to speak and to teach, to develop their own theory in the light of others' creative responses. All of this assumes the position we suggested earlier: that workers are themselves active, both theoretically and practically, as subjects of history.

At the same time, Marxism must involve the kind of ruthless realism that Eley seems to find objectionable in Lenin. If the ruling class has an interest in shaping the inner world of movement organisation, ideas and activity, then at any time the movement as a whole may include forces whose practice and ideas work to mediate ruling class ideas within the movement.[64] The implication of that should be very clear: one part of the movement is a problem for the left, and needs to be opposed effectively. Thus issues of strategy and tactics concern the interior life of movements. It is necessary to differentiate within 'the left' between left and right, with the right understood as *systematically* opposed to working class revolution, ie in the strict sense counter-revolutionary. At best, the right within the movement is always an unreliable ally, and may come to adopt completely the standpoint of capital and the state.

That was a key lesson Marx derived from the experience of the 1848 revolutions. Later Marxists would further elaborate the practical implications. The left must establish its own organisational and ideological identity, separate from and opposed to the 'moderate' wing within movements. It needs to do this so that, at any juncture, it has the capacity to clarify the critical questions facing the movement, and to argue from within for the adoption of its own strategy and tactics, as against those whose alternative leadership would mislead it. The left must stand ready, always, to take sides in intra-movement disputes and debates, and make continuous reassessments of successive situations in terms of their particular limits and potentialities.

A Marxist politics understood in these terms is not 'revolutionism at any price'. It demands careful assessment of the balance of forces at any given moment both within and between movements and their class opponents. It demands the kind of practical judgment displayed, for example, by the Bolsheviks in the 'July Days' in Petrograd when, faced with a vast armed demonstration of sailors, soldiers and workers, they were able to say 'Not yet' to insurrectionary calls—on the grounds that a majority of workers, let alone others, were *not yet* convinced of the necessity of a second revolution. That same capacity to judge the situation and act accordingly was, tragically, absent from the German Spartacists and the Hungarian communists in 1919. Practical Marxism never meant abstention from specific struggles. As Lukács argued, against his 'Menshevist' opponents, the defeat in Hungary occurred, not because 'historical processes' did not allow victory, but because—in essence—the new Hungarian Communist Party 'blew it' through inexperience.[65] It was precisely the capacity to make serious assessments of situations, and then to intervene actively and effectively, that Lenin, Trotsky and the best leaders of the new Communist International attempted to instill in their comrades in post-war Western Europe.

In the event, they failed. But for several years it was a close-run thing. The consequences of the failure would mark the rest of the 20th century. There followed a whole series of political crises in which the possibility of significant revolutionary intervention was posed. But by the mid-1920s those who held to the tenets of Bolshevism had been marginalised. For the rest of the century, they did not achieve implantation in Europe's movements to shape their development. They could and did provide a series of often brilliant commentaries on events, demonstrating the dangers and the bankruptcies of other tendencies, and outlines of how things might have been different—but without the practical capacity to see their standpoint win out.

Social democracy proved, time and again, incapable of responding adequately to major crises or, worse, it played a conservative role—in a pattern already established in the period before, during and after the First World War. What was new was the evolution of the official communist movement. The Russian Revolution's isolation, along with the multiple defeats and mistakes across Europe in the early years after 1917-1918, produced the conditions for a conservative 'degeneration' of the Russian regime and, in parallel, of the guidance it provided to communist parties elsewhere. The internationalism of 1917 was replaced, by the mid-1920s, by the predominance of Stalin's doctrine of 'socialism in one country', and an increasing subordination of the international communist movement to the *raison d'état* of the Russian state. Official communist policy would veer and zigzag in all manner of directions over subsequent decades, but never in a direction that involved the development of a consistent revolutionary policy based on real working class power.

Geoff Eley provides much of the materials from which it would be possible to assemble this argument about post-1923 European developments, and in that sense his book is useful as a source for mining by socialists. But he doesn't offer the argument itself. The revolutionary left rather disappears from view in the rest of his history—and thus also in his prognoses for the future.

1924-1967

The inter-war years turned into disaster both for the left and for democracy in Europe. Social democracy collapsed in the face of economic crisis, Stalinism triumphed in the USSR, the Nazis came to power in Germany and then Austria, the Spanish republic was defeated, and the world was plunged into the even more barbarous slaughter of the Second World War. Eley's book is unevenly helpful in understanding these dreadful defeats.

He's at his best dissecting the weaknesses of social democracy. Organised reformism had emerged in a seemingly stronger position once the years of revolutionary crisis had passed. Nowhere did this seem more true than in 'Red Vienna'. Yet, as he notes, there was a 'reformist conundrum' underlying the Austrian socialists' achievements: 'they depended ultimately on a prosperous capitalism,' and they had no strategy for transcending capitalism's limits:

The labour movement wielded impressive social power, as a subcultural complex organising the community solidarity and everyday lives of the working class in all the ways Red Vienna professed. Yet the bridge from this subaltern collectivism to genuine political leadership over society—hegemony in Gramsci's sense—had yet to be found. Translating the labour movement's subcultural influence into power in the state, through a non-insurrectionary revolutionary strategy, was the problem.[66]

Reformism's key theorists completely misestimated their prospects. Hilferding argued that capitalism was now 'organised', making democratic public control of the economy easier. Napthali and others developed what they claimed was an alternative strategy to Leninism, in which either reformism was capable of having revolutionary consequences or (as Kautsky argued), since capitalism automatically led to socialisation, socialists should do no more than encourage capitalism's maturation. As Eley notes, 'This reliance on capitalism's future foundered in the 1929 crash'.[67] The German SPD accepted huge cuts in social spending and wages, believing it more important to restore capitalism's profitability than to hasten its demise. They backed Germany's conservative forces, chiefly because of their fear of the Nazis, 'while the socialist rank and file suffered creeping demoralisation'.[68] Eley's summary of social democracy's stance is correct:

> Having rejected the Bolsheviks' vanguardist model of proletarian democracy as authoritarian and counter-productive, a recipe for destructive violence and self isolating dictatorship, social democrats adhered rigidly to parliamentary rules, trapped in a psychology of proceduralism and forever shying from the fight. This hardwiring of social democratic imaginations into the integrated circuits of parliamentary legality was the key to the post-1918 period.[69]

Faced with the threat of Nazism, the social democrats adhered, to the bitter end, to their parliamentary cretinism, leaving their own rank and file, many of whom were ready to fight, leaderless and demoralised. Given their whole previous history, that was hardly surprising. The problem in Germany was that no force to the SPD's left had a policy capable of pulling whole sections of the SPD's membership into joint anti-Nazi activity. And here the question of the Communist Party, and the whole problem of Stalinism, is critical.

What is extraordinary about Eley's treatment of this question is that he has almost nothing to say about it. Famously, the German Communist Party, following Stalin's lead, declared that the German social democrats were not potential allies in resistance to the Nazis but 'social fascists', enemies of the working class equivalent to Hitler's forces. The KPD pursued a lunatic 'ultra-left' course, splitting rather than uniting the German workers' movement. But Eley has nothing to say about the political effects of the theory and practice of the Stalinist 'Third Period', or indeed about the processes by which the Nazis came to power in Germany in 1933. He only notes that their 'seizure of power' was a disaster for the left, a 'democratic catastrophe'.[70] Nowhere does he consider the respective roles of the SPD and the KPD in allowing this catastrophe. If ever there was a case where events, and the responsibility of various left forces for outcomes, demanded analysis, this surely was it. But Eley—a notable historian of Germany—offers *nothing*. If his lapse over Mussolini's victory was weird, his silence over Hitler's victory, in a history of the left and democracy, is an unbelievable error.

Eley's treatment of Stalinism presents problems. The distance between Eley and the tradition represented by this journal comes out in a choice of phrase: '*Revolutionary agency* was exercised on gargantuan scale in the Soviet industrialisation drive after 1929, as *Bolsheviks* transformed their society from above' (my emphases).[71] Given that the Stalinist industrialisation drive was premised on massive cuts in workers' wages, the reversal of peasants' land gains in the 1917 revolution, and the extirpation of any last remnants of soviet democracy, the term 'counter-revolutionary agency' seems more appropriate; while any notion of serious political continuity between the *revolutionary* Bolsheviks and Stalin's Communist apparatchiks seems more than dubious. While Eley offers some bare facts concerning the USSR, European Communists' uncritical identification with its rulers, their policies and purges, and the failures of the Popular Front and the Stalin-Hitler Pact, he never offers any serious account of why and how events in Russian happened as they did, and why the history of the 20th century left is therefore so tragic. Yet the matter is significant for his theme: were Russia's rulers always in some sense part of the left, or did they transmute into something else, to become part of the problem facing the left? Did they indeed, as this journal's tradition has argued, become part of the ruling class of modern world capitalism? If the former, then the story of the left must be told in one way; if the latter, the history must be told differently. Eley doesn't pose the question, but his failure to do so makes for an incoherent history that seems to straddle both positions without recognising its own dilemmas.

Our tendency has argued for more than half a century that the degeneration of the Russian Revolution of 1917 did produce a qualitative shift to a form of capitalist class society. The implication is, then, that Stalin and his heirs, and their policies, are only part of the story of the left in two senses. First, they developed as a significant part of world capitalism, with which the left had to interact and which it had to oppose. Second, however, large forces on the left failed to recognise that situation, with immensely confusing and demoralising effects that revealed themselves time and again. This is, in principle, quite as open to analysis as the dependence of the German social democrats on the old regime, the existence of many Tory voters within the ranks of the British working class, and so on. The influence of Stalinism in working class and 'progressive' politics across the world for two generations became nothing other than a case of the normal dominance of ruling class ideas over the consciousness of the exploited and oppressed—with the difference, of course, that the ruling class in question happened to be abroad. Such a perspective makes it easier to understand how, probably from the adoption of 'socialism in one country' in 1924 and the debacles of the British General Strike and the Chinese Revolution, through the 'Third Period', and most certainly from the adoption of the Popular Front onwards, 'communism' became a politics which first *failed to threaten* capitalism and eventually—via Eurocommunism and its successors—turned into a politics that embraced capitalism in the name of 'realism'. Along the way, 'communism' in Europe became, like social democracy, in practice *counter-revolutionary* in the strict sense that it opposed popular revolution—in Spain during 1936 and after, in Eastern Europe and Western Europe from 1944, in Hungary in 1956, in France in May 1968, etc. Eley is too good a historian not to record the transitions empirically. But he does not account for them. That failure makes his history far less interesting and useful than it might have been.

Eley's history is better on the politics of the Popular Front in France and in Spain, where he catches the subordination of class politics to national politics. On France, he notes the revival of the direct action spirit of 1917-1921, and the élan that accompanied this. However, the Blum government wagered—like the Austrian social democrats of the 1920s—on capitalist success to fund their programmes, and then had no answer when capital went on strike, abandoning its commitments and cutting back its social legislation. Even here, Eley has no sense of the need for an 'eventful' history, in which the responses of different players are analysed and explained at each juncture, and in which it is possible to explore the kind of left interventions that were needed. The sharpest light needs to fall on the French Communist Party, as the most left wing of the forces involved. However, beyond noting rightly that the PCF 'sought to leash militancy as much as drive it on', Eley tells us little.[72] He offers a summary answer to the question, how might the debacle in France have been avoided?

> This situation needed leaders of vision who commanded the necessary political will—capitalising on the opening of June 1936, feeding the sense of historic opportunity, driving the advantage home against the dominant classes, and finding the broadest unity in the PCF's sense.[73]

But if this is what was needed, what would it have demanded of, say, the leaders of the PCF—given that such leadership would never have come from the SFIO or the Radicals? In the real world, any such leadership of vision must always be constructed in the face and teeth of other, non-visionary leaderships within popular movements, and that implies a struggle inside movements between rival tendencies. Either such a struggle can be pursued with clarity, along lines indicated by the earlier remarks about 'Leninism', or it can be evaded in the spurious interests of an abstract 'unity' which involves conceding the struggle to those who would moderate and disable the movement.[74] How could or should the left have responded to crises like the strike of capital? What would it mean in practice to 'drive the advantage home against the dominant classes'? One feature would have to be further moves towards socialisation, surely—and that would have involved, indeed demanded, the further mobilisation of workers in the factories and mines, etc. A logic akin to that of '1917' would have supervened—against Stalin's wishes, to be sure, and going far beyond the limiting logic of the Popular Front. Popular mobilisations like that in France in 1936 develop in one of two directions: either forward, to an institutional remaking of politics and society that depends on the mobilising power of millions, or backwards, to their own demobilisation and demoralisation, and to a recuperation of ruling class positions—sometimes at deadly cost. That choice of direction appears at critical turning points in each movement's development, when the balance of forces within the movement as well as between itself and its opponents is tested. Specific moments and events *matter*. The experience of two centuries of mass movements suggests that, even if each movement has its own historical particularities, there is a kind of inescapable logic to these moments of dilemma, and a left that is unable to respond decisively to them declares its irrelevance or worse.

The Spanish Civil War produced yet another terrible defeat for the left and for democracy. Eley offers sufficient materials to show what a disaster the Popular Front was, both in Spain itself and internationally, though he offers no suggestions about what alternative policies were required. Though he's correct, it's not enough to say, 'Prosecuting the war with a central command while securing the revolutionary gains were not mutually exclusive'.[75] As he says, the whole Popular Front strategy failed. That might suggest that he would argue for some alternative, but he doesn't. He writes of Spain:

> The Comintern hoped to combine both the United Front of working class parties and the broader Popular Front... But many divisions undermined the effort. The biggest of these pitted the Comintern's advocacy of self limiting republican defence, from which specifically socialist demands were dropped, against the desires of the people militant, for whom revolution was all.[76]

That 'pitting' (as he records) included the Comintern's and the GPU's use of terror against the POUM, etc 'in a disgraceful copy of the Soviet purges'.[77] From all of this, who could and should learn what? In particular, who on the left should learn what? While history may have been 'bunk' for Henry Ford, for socialists it can at least be a book of shocking lessons. But Eley doesn't draw any.

All in all, the 1930s were a dreadful decade for the left, only to be followed by the barbarity of the Second World War. Perhaps the 'midnight of the century' was provided by Stalin, not just entering a (soon to be dissolved) non-aggression pact with Hitler that included the carving up of Poland between them, but actually handing over German Communists to the Gestapo's tender mercies as a terrible coda to 'socialism in one country'.

The death toll and destructiveness of the war were appalling, yet the reformist left did manage to make some gains—not so much by its own actions as a result of the Allies' final compulsion to contain the fascist powers of Germany and Italy and also the Japanese empire. In their victory, the Allies remade the world's political map, constructing new empires in place of the old and redividing the world on new lines. That new world, by accident rather than design, then entered a period of unparalleled growth and prosperity for a quarter of a century.[78]

Eley suggests there was a brief moment at the end of the war when other possibilities seemed to open up:

> The left's situation in 1945 was close to what the 1935 Popular Front strategy had imagined. The international coalition against fascism had worked. Mussolini was deposed, Hitler defeated; of the other rightist dictators only Franco in Spain and…Salazar in Portugal remained. The 'workers' state', the Soviet Union, had emerged triumphantly from a war that had immensely boosted its prestige. Broad coalitions for democracy and reform, so called national fronts, were formed in most countries. United fronts between Socialists and Communists were also common, especially locally all over Europe. Radical changes seemed afoot.[79]

However, as he says, 'the chance was fleeting'—it lasted at most from 1943 to 1947. He dubs those years the 'moment of anti-fascist unity', which he sees as a period of 'radical openness'. My feeling is that Eley rather exaggerates the potential of this moment. His argument is that the Resistance organs in France, Italy and elsewhere represented the seeds of a more democratic and participatory alternative, and that their disbanding and disarming—under Communist Party pressure especially—was a key defeat. 'These were', he proposes, 'the molecular forms of a different course, analogous to the workers' councils that mushroomed across Europe in 1917-1921. Both movements aspired to remake society in just and egalitarian ways, organising food supplies, social administration, and public order in the end of the war emergency, while enlisting ordinary people's energies and skills.' Eley comments, by now characteristically, that what was lost was 'the chance for creative *intermediate solutions*…for harnessing the energy, idealism, and commitment of the people in motion, by building new participatory forms into emerging constitutional settlements, bridging the gap between national arenas and the local everyday' (my emphasis).[80] The difficulty is that the comparison with the end of the 1914-1918 war goes only so far. First, the scale of anti-fascist committees' organising capacity, their rootedness in popular militancy and their connections to both workplace strength and military mutinies were very much less; second, nowhere were significant political forces capable of harnessing the undoubted radical moods at the end of the war for really transformative purposes, in competition with the demobilising policies of both the Communist and social democratic parties. In Britain, nationalisation was, as he says, 'the socialisation of loss not profit' and lacking any real socialist content.[81] In his judgment, 'participation was the democratic fault-line of the post-war settlements in Western Europe… [There was] a sad contraction of the democratic imagination. Politics was squeezed back into parliamentary frames; other forms were forgotten'.[82]

The US played a key role in the post-war conservative consolidation of Western Europe at the same time that, in Eastern Europe, Moscow's conservative ascendancy was brutally enforced. All across Europe, even if by different means and even if in ways that promoted popular living standards, labour remained firmly subordinated to renewed capital accumulation.

1968 and after

'There is not much enthusiasm abroad among intellectuals in our time', wrote the (then) Trotskyist Alasdair MacIntyre in 1960, 'for the day when the last king will be strangled with the entrails of the last priest'.[83] For more than two decades after 1945, revolutionary (indeed, even radical) ideas were the property only of tiny isolated sects—the *groupuscules* that Charles de Gaulle derided (even as he banned them) in 1968. The predominant conservative consensus, denying the possibility of radical social change, affected even leading thinkers on the left. The most that happened in the 1950s and early 1960s was a degree of repositioning among the radical left: in particular, the brutal crushing of the 1956 Hungarian Revolution undermined the hegemony of Communist parties on the left, and independent 'new' lefts played significant roles in, for example, French opposition to the Algerian war and in the growth of CND in Britain. Two decades of full employment bred a new degree of confidence among shopfloor workers, represented by a rising tide of unofficial and wildcat strike action. In addition, though Eley doesn't mention this, a number of important impulses crossed the Atlantic to Europe. The civil rights movement in the US not only seized the imagination of European radicals, but also provided the seedbed for several other important developments. The student movement, which rapidly developed open opposition to the US war in Vietnam, the first stirrings of a new women's movement, some of the earliest critiques of capitalist ecology, and (a little later) new gay and lesbian liberation movements all spread east from the US, to take on their own local colours and forms across Europe.

These and other impulses came together in the extraordinary explosion in France in 1968—also the year of the Tet offensive, of the birth of the civil rights movement in Ireland, and of much more. May-June 1968 initiated a new period in the history of the left. Eley provides a lively narrative of the May events, observing about the crisis that followed the workers' rejection of the Grenelle agreements:

> The gap between the popular movement and the left's existing national leaderships now really mattered. The former had no national structure. Ideal for some purposes, anti-centralism was disabling in a general crisis of the state.[84]

He goes on to discuss the government's use of its centralised forces to attack those strikers who continued, and equally the way that the centralised French Communist Party stepped up its denunciations of the students. Yet he draws no general lesson that might inform the rest of his history of the last third of the 20th century. What he does say is that 'two lefts faced each other across the frontier of de Gaulle's 30 May address— one anxiously awaiting normal politics to return, the other disbelieving they ever could'.[85] On one side was an 'old left' typified by the PCF, and marked by conservatism; on the other was a 'new left' marked by anti-authoritarianism and the ideal of self management. I'm not sure that Eley draws the line of division very accurately. The 'old left', he suggests, spoke of 'seizing power in the state' while the new left spoke of beginning with a change in everyday life. These ideas are what marks the post-1968 period from what went before:

> From the fascination with direct democracy and participatory forms through 'permissiveness' to the enabling of sexuality and the counter-culture's hedonistic excess, from the practical experiments with autogestion to the obsessive critiques of alienation—in all these respects '1968' challenged the hegemony of '1945'. The resulting conflicts took many years to work themselves out,

but over the longer term their effects were huge. They redefined the ground of politics. They complicated notions of the left. They changed established assumptions about where radical democratic agency could be found.[86]

Eley's terminology is ambiguous: the old left's concern, to 'seize power in the state', might mean seizing state power through revolution and might mean contesting elections in order to obtain a modicum of state office. In reality the French Communist Party (and other essentially reformist parties) saved the language of 'revolution' for May Day purposes—though Eley, oddly, refers later to the (by then, Eurocommunist) parties of Italy, France and Spain as 'the last organised advocacy of revolutionary socialism in Western Europe',[87] rather ignoring the fact that they had ceased to take such positions seriously since the 1920s! It might be more illuminating to see the dividing line between the conservatism of an old left and the radicalism of a new left as an issue between a politics from above and from below. Among the new left there continued to be a quite fluid debate about the appropriateness of continuing with the language of 'revolution'. Parts of the 'new left' proved perfectly capable of stepping back across the divide and rejoining the 'old left' (in the shape of the Communist and social democratic parties). The new feminism or sexual permissiveness, for example, was not automatically linked to anti-authoritarianism or to ideals of self management.

That the 'ground of politics' changed in important respects is undeniable. Part of that involved a major (re)discovery of the politics of gender and sexuality—the issue that most exercises Eley. The very idea of socialism was hugely enriched by this. But equally, an increasingly urgent critique of capitalist *ecology* reshaped socialist thought, even if Eley has less to say about this. His focus on matters posed by feminism means that he rather downplays the importance of issues to do with immigration, racism and the revival of fascism across Europe. He records the importance of racial and other divisions, but remarks that 'left parties largely evaded the challenge of this popular divisiveness',[88] which rather lets those parties off the hook. In reality, they *promoted* racist division via tightened immigration controls and the acceptance of arguments about 'acceptable numbers' of immigrants. That 'New Labour' under Blair and Blunkett has been even worse than 'Old Labour' is beside the point: Old Labour adopted shamefully racist positions from 1965 onwards,[89] while Communist parties accepted the 'need' for immigration controls, urging only that these should be 'non-racist'—whatever that meant!

Despite his attention to 'second-wave feminism', I suspect that Eley actually underestimates its impact. He writes that it 'failed to institutionalise itself nationally',[90] but doesn't allow for another possibility, which is that the women's movement did succeed, to adapt an idea from Edward Thompson, in warrening society from end to end, even if like the 19th century workers' movement it did not achieve its multiple ends.[91] If there was one part of society it warrened with particular success, it was the European left, many of whose fundamental assumptions about 'class', 'democracy' and the like were reshaped after the 1960s under its pressure.

Where Eley parts company with our tradition most seriously is in his discussion of 'class and the politics of labour'.[92] In essence, he offers a version of Hobsbawm's arguments about 'the forward march of labour halted'. Where, in the past, he suggests, the socialist project was tied to an idea of the centrality of the working class, itself rooted in 'Fordism' (in essence, big factories and Keynesianism), now that very basis of identification has gone, along with the working class itself as a political formation. Eley concedes that 'class as an analytical category, and as an organising condition of social life, may have remained' (I like that *may*!), and indeed he is also correct that 'its structure and manifest forms had profoundly changed'.[93] It's true that 'with new employment patterns, the geography and gender of working-classness changed, as did the architecture of everyday life in housing, family, sexuality, friendship, schooling, recreation and leisure, and taste and style. So too did the cultures of identification. It made a difference if the representative trade unionists were coal miners, dockers, steel workers, machine builders, and other men applying muscle and intelligence to arduous physical tasks, or men and women sitting behind computers, canteen or laundry workers in public institutions, or nurses' aids in big city hospitals. The valencies of class as a basis for politics were different'.[94] But so what? And how is that different from the 'cultures of identification' of the 1930s in the new car and aircraft (mostly men) and light engineering (mostly women) factories, which were initially seen as inherently closed spaces for trade unionism, yet later viewed as central bastions of labour militancy (and indeed of safe Labour voting)? In the end, the whole argument comes down to this: is the place of class struggle in the battle for socialism altered by ongoing sociological and cultural changes within capitalism by, as it were, 'structural' shifts in the occupational composition of the working class, or is the politics of the class struggle far more decisive? If, as Eley is inclined to think, 'class' as a basis for socialist politics is finished, what on earth does 'socialism' now mean? Are we to assume that the politics of 'new social movements' are to take the place of class-based radical politics? Eley, picking up a widespread notion in the 1980s and 1990s, is inclined to think that way. The view is one he shares with the former Communist intellectuals who went on to establish (and then dissolve) *Marxism Today* in Britain, and who gave intellectual expression to the drift of much of the European left away from 'ultra-leftism' and towards an accommodation first with social democracy and increasingly 'market socialism' and indeed just 'marketism'.

The root of Eley's view is a kind of sociological determinism, which also underpinned much of the uncritical celebration of 'new social movements' in the 1980s and 1990s.[95] Eley inclines that way:

> By the 1970s, the left had a central problem. As parties traditionally based on the industrial working class, socialists and Communists were appealing to ever smaller populations. Furthermore, the remaining workers no longer saw themselves collectively in the same way. As an operative identity—as the socialist tradition's organising myth, capable of inspiring collective action, of uniting disparate categories of working people inside the same solidarity, with enduring efficacy in politics—the 'working class' was losing its motive power.
>
> In this double sense—in social structure and social understandings, as the social aggregation of wage-earning positions in industrial economies and as an organised political entity—the working class declined.[96]

True, he immediately adds, one kind of worker was being replaced by another—Eley is too sophisticated to fall for a general thesis of 'deproletarianisation'—but nonetheless he identifies an 'unmaking' of the working class where previously there had been a 'making' (to borrow again from Thompson). And the logic underpinning that unmaking is a semi-structural one.

There is an alternative account, which in my view makes far better sense of the last three decades.[97] The great wave of popular struggle that climaxed in Europe in the late 1960s and early 1970s ran into essentially *political* barriers produced by the continued dominance of social democratic and official Communist politics. It subsided, and its decline was registered above all in terms of industrial struggle. What contained and then pushed back working class militancy was not immediately a direct offensive by capital and states, but the collaborationist politics of union leaders and the parties to which they were tied. Here our interpretation of the 1970s differs very sharply from Eley's. For him, the Social Contract between the unions and the Labour government of the 1970s was given 'some much-needed social idealism and ethical drive' by Jack Jones of the TGWU.[98] Eley makes no mention of the way both Jones and the other major 'left' union leader at the time, Hugh Scanlon, encouraged scabbing, or of the fact that the British left (both the International Socialists and the CP!) *campaigned against* the Social Contract. Even his account of the decline of union membership has to be qualified. The TUC's weakness in Britain is explained in terms of 'the politics of a virulent anti-union drive'[99] as if that determined the TUC weakness, rather than its own bankrupt 'new realism', whose path had already been prepared by the same Jones and Scanlon. None of the major defeats that working class organisation undoubtedly suffered in the 1980s was somehow inscribed in automatic social processes. Perhaps the greatest of those defeats, that inflicted on the British miners, was quite as 'resistible' as fascism's victories in the inter-war years. Both problems in the strike's leadership, and failures by other union leaderships in the delivery of solidarity action created the conditions for Thatcher's victory over the miners.[100]

Recovery from periods of defeat is a drawn out process, requiring a regrowth of confidence, sometimes the emergence of a new generation less marked by the scars of old battles, but should not be confused with some terminal decline due to a change in the occupational composition of the working class.[101] That there was a 'downturn' in working class combativity from the mid-1970s onwards is undeniable,[102] but the sense we make of that period of retreat and defeat must necessarily shape our whole political conception of what is possible and necessary, and what the future may hold. Eley's rather deterministic position leads him to look for substitutes for working class power as an agency of transformation, and thus not to consider the possibility of a revival of working class organisation and militancy. He does not, for example, take serious note of the huge public sector strikes in France in 1995, nor does his whole account prepare the reader for the large strike waves in Italy, Greece and Spain in the context of the anti-war movement of the past year and more. What he draws is a contrast between a rather rosy past and a grim present:

Through these changes trade unionism lost its credentials as a progressive force. Unions had always been intimately connected with socialism. Beyond party-union relations was the larger sense of trade unionism as the weapon of the weak, mobilising workers' collectively organised strength as their only defence against exploitation, social inequalities, and the power of capital. Trade unionism was a class capacity, through which masses acting in unison could have effects. Industrial strength was essential for immediate improvement in wages and working conditions. But trade unionism was also a larger vision, a collectivist ideal of the general good, a desire for improving society, a general ethic of social solidarity.

...Under welfare states, however, trade unionism stopped carrying these hopes of the poor...mainly trade unionism narrowed into sectionalism.[103]

One would not guess from this account that sectionalism had ever been a problem in the past, and certainly not that trade union history involves a dialectic of sectionalism and collectivism. The history of trade unionism includes the engineers, who only admitted women to membership in 1940, and even then in a special 'section'. Nor was sectional strength always a necessarily backward feature, standing against the possibility of class identification: witness the deployment of craft union strength in the shop stewards' movement of the First World War.

By the 1990s, in Eley's account, 'the left was divided between advocates of change and defenders of the faith. The former carried the day'.[104] By 1990, it would be more accurate to say that his 'advocates of change' were giving up entirely on the possibility of change, *conceding* victory to capitalism. That the left—'defenders of the faith'—were very weak in 1990 is true, but it will hardly do to place them in the camp of sad conservatives, unable to see that the world had changed. It was not from the ranks of the 'advocates of change', after all, that the new movements against global capitalism at the turn of the new century would come; the 'defenders of the faith' embraced them readily.

Yet Eley also continues to provide good materials on this final period. As so often, he is at his best documenting the failures of reformist parties. He notes the way that the Eurocommunist strategy in Italy ran into the sand, as the PCI (the Italian Communist Party) became 'the party of law and order, the bulwark of democratic legality, the shield of the constitution'—only this was a bulwark and shield defending a corrupt state still honeycombed with

DC vested interests, and a well-oiled machinery of paybacks and private enrichment. Restricting public rights and expanding police powers, the PCI's anti-terrorist stance painfully compromised its guardianship of civil liberties. By its strong alignment with the DC, the PCI damaged its links to the broader left. 'In the Historic Compromise, the PCI rehearsed an old socialist dilemma, familiar from Weimar and Red Vienna. By accepting the system's premises—NATO, the DC, Catholicism, and capitalism—the PCI took a deck already stacked'.[105] Like Jones and Scanlon in Britain, they espoused a version of the Social Contract, on the theory that workers' sacrifices would save the economy and enable its reconstitution on more equitable bases, linked to social reforms and stronger democracy. What the theory meant in practice was demobilise your own side, and expect to gain reforms! As Eley says, 'By 1979, there was little to show for this compromising. Inflation was down to 12.4 percent, and unions made big concessions on wage indexing, redundancies, and productivity. But unemployment was rising and workers' dissatisfaction was rife'.[106] In Spain, too, the Communist Party pursued the politics of 'pacts', and lost out to a revived social democratic party, the PSOE. In France they did no better. Eley credits Eurocommunism with some civil reforms, and also with a truly ambiguous achievement: 'Eurocommunism brought southern Europe into the fold of social democracy'.[107] Despite its failures, he is warm to Eurocommunism: in making 'broader appeals to socially diverse support, from new professionals and white collar strata to the university-educated and women', the CPs:

> ...implied a different kind of party from before—*away* from the Leninist party of militants, with its demands of time and energy, and exclusive Communist loyalties; and *toward* the broadly campaigning electoral party, with its looser structure of alliances and less exacting identification, based on varied social constituencies. Eurocommunist calls to democratise the party meant not only dismantling centralism but also opening the party to diverse currents and issues. Such issues posed a distinct challenge for parties of the left, given their powerful class-political reflexes. *This* agenda remained on the table.
>
> Finally, Eurocommunism opened greater space on the left for radical democracy, suggesting a 'third way' between Western European social democracy and the official Communisms of the East.[108]

Here Eley's inexhaustible search for a 'third way' leads him seriously astray. Eurocommunism represented a further shift to the right in Western Europe, with the rhetoric of 'radical democracy' as a partial cover. Moreover, the idea that some desirable path could be found *between* a rightward moving social democracy and a decaying Stalinism is hardly full of attractions for any kind of left!

Part of the difficulty is that, as we noted above, Eley never really comes to terms with Stalinism. Its crisis in the 1980s leaves him somewhat adrift. He continues to allow the use of the term 'socialist' in relation to Russia and Eastern Europe.[109] True, many on the left in the West still maintained all manner of illusions and identifications with the USSR and its satellites, but Eley never gets behind this to consider its effects. As a result, he has some difficulty with the explosions in Eastern Europe. While he notes, rightly, that Solidarity in Poland 'belonged squarely within socialist traditions' even while its ideas had great difficulty in finding expression in socialist language, and while he can properly record that 'it was certainly Europe's most impressive working class insurgency since 1917-23', for him the outcome in Jaruzelski's declaration of martial law was 'inevitable'.[110] Sadly, he allows the Italian Communist Party to draw the moral from Solidarity's defeat:

> We must accept that this phase of socialist development (which began with the October Revolution) has exhausted its driving force, just as the phase which saw the birth and development of socialist parties and trade union movements mustered around the Socialist International also ran out of steam…[111]

His halfway treatment of the nature of Stalinist societies leaves Eley with an unanswered question: if these societies were in some sense socialist, then isn't his whole book's stated theme that there is a profound connection between socialism and democracy flawed? Also, two things need to be explained about the East European revolutions of 1989. First, why was there a low level of 'social movement' involvement, for example by comparison with the Solidarity period in Poland, 1980-1981? Second, why did the new governments embrace the market so eagerly?

On the first, he writes with some accuracy that—outside Romania—the common organisational medium of the revolutions was 'the Forum', which he describes thus: 'a broad informal front, hastily improvised, comprising mainly intellectuals, with unclear popular support and not representative in any procedurally democratic sense…self constituted committees'. Yet he treats these as somehow embodying 'revived civil societies where democracy could be regrounded, the sites of a "parallel polis";' and he writes, 'The intense moment of the revolution as an immediate event was an extraordinary laboratory of popular democratic initiative—especially in the massed insurgencies of Czechoslovakia and the GDR but also in the popular ferment of the negotiated transitions as well, and in every small and everyday statement of rebellion across the region'.[112] There's a contradiction here, which Eley doesn't explore properly. Something was 'missing' in 1989, and it was surely any popular institutional initiative, itself a necessary component of popular democratic insurgency. The Forums were a way of avoiding this: in Poland, Lech Walesa was explicit about the matter, declaring it a matter of principle that 'the street' should be excluded from the negotiations. The East European revolutions had something in common with the 'negotiated transitions' in Spain, in Argentina and Brazil, etc: the people were largely excluded, except when called on to participate in mass demonstrations. In the GDR, indeed, the people seem to have explicitly rejected the politics of the Civic Forum, and its class-bound assumptions.[113]

On the second question, Eley perceives a 'painful dilemma for the left' in the way that post-Communist governments shared a neo-liberal belief in privatisation and marketisation. He comments, 'Private property, the market, capitalism—these were what socialists wanted to overturn. Socialist readiness to embrace the market, not in some Keynesian sense of the mixed economy but in a more absolute sense, was a profound change. It became the common ground of Eastern European reform'.[114] That it became 'common ground' is certainly true. But 'socialist readiness'? Surely the point is that there were never revolutions in which specifically *socialist* ideas were less prevalent? The intelligentsia, by and large, had given up on socialism, in any meaning of the term. Thinking that Stalinism was socialism, and seeing the 'socialism' of social democracy as anyway largely empty and lacking in moral vigour, they bought the neo-liberal idea that 'freedom' was indissolubly linked to the market. If critical Marxist voices were thin on the ground in the West, they were even thinner in the East. The few there had been (notably Kuron and Modzelewski in Poland) had long abandoned their own revolutionary ideas; the Yugoslav Marxists (and *Praxis*) had gone silent or converted to nationalism. Eley writes of the 'shock therapy' applied across the region, 'This was less the transition to democracy than the region's brutal subjection to the global capitalist system'.[115]

His phrasing would have been clearer if, in place of 'less... than', he had said 'both... and', forcing the paradox to the surface, and compelling inquiry into both the conditions that permitted such an association to persist for a time and that, in the longer run, would draw people from Eastern Europe into the anti-capitalist demonstrations in Prague, Genoa and so on.

Eley's account of the 1990s begins—rather peculiarly, given that he has just recorded a whole series of revolutions in Eastern Europe—by suggesting that the days of insurrection are past, 'the popular uprising, a pitched battle for the state amid the sudden collapse of the system'. That he has a poor understanding of insurrections is suggested by his comment that the 'storming of the Winter Palace' was the emblematic event of the October Revolution in Russia. After 1917, he thinks, insurgencies became rare: 'There was one case of popular insurrection under late capitalism, namely France in 1968, where liberal democracy was brought to a halt. And the revolutions of 1989 produced systemic change on a transnational scale. But otherwise, the insurrectionary fantasy—of a massed uprising, paralysing government and violently seizing power—largely disappeared'.[116] The whole account is a bit fantastical. First, outside the imagination of movie-makers, there was never a 'storming of the Winter Palace', which was actually taken by a tiny group who slipped in through the back door. Nor was there, as Eley's own earlier account shows, an 'insurrection' in France in 1968. That any serious idea of socialist revolution has little in common with Eley's fantasies needs stressing: its 'emblematic events' are more likely to involve workers' self organisation, often of a non-murderous kind, and not all at once, but as a spreading and deepening movement combining economic and political demands that pulls into its orbit all manner of other struggles against oppression and the like.

Never mind. That was the fantasy, says Eley, and in his account the disappointments of 1968 led some student radicals to chase it, recreating the Leninist model 'in the form of small and hyperdisciplined sects, rejecting participatory ideals for the panacea of the party'. I don't know what company Eley kept, but that was anything but universally true. That many leftists lapsed into sectarianism is correct, but not all did. Perhaps what he terms 'sectarian militancy was thus little more than a noisy sideshow', but he needs at least to get his facts right about it. He has a footnote saying that 'Wishfully, the Socialist Labour League and International Socialists declared Britain pre-revolutionary, launching respectively the Workers Revolutionary Party (1973) and the Socialist Workers Party (1976), each reaching a membership of several thousand'.[117] If we leave aside the SLL/WRP, which was rather prone to declare every temporary blip a terminal crisis, the IS/SWP never declared Britain pre-revolutionary, and changed its name for much more mundane reasons. But Eley, who has little time for the revolutionary left, doesn't bother to do his homework properly here.

He's inclined to hope that 'DIY' politics as exemplified by raves, roads protests and Reclaim the Streets might offer part of a way forward. Tentatively he suggests that some modest kind of 'localism' in economic policy might enable socialist ideas to regain ground lost to neo-liberalism, and partly reclaim collectivism:

> Modified Keynesianism was feasible—involving decentralised public enterprise, tax concessions and public funds for local initiatives, use of public resources like land and planning permission for smaller-scale projects, community-based planning, none of which meant reversing privatisation or relegitimising nationalisation per se.[118]

However, in a 'brutally adversarial national climate', those backing such ideas—like the GLC of the 1980s—were overwhelmed. The outcome was the 'confusing picture' he finds at the end of his story, in the late 1990s. 'Socialists were governing almost everywhere', he suggests, adding, however, that these 'socialists returned to office with no economic design'[119]—a judgement that is breathtakingly misdirected, certainly as far as Britain is concerned. Blair and his 'New Labour' government had a definite economic design, taken over and developed from essentially Thatcherite ideas, and they eschewed completely even the language of socialism. In Germany, an official SPD intellectual declared that 'the left must stand up for consumer rights, free investment decisions, the free disposal of assets, and a decentralised decision making process'.[120] The 'established socialist tradition' had been left behind, capitalism's ascendant forms were embraced, and the rule of the market was accepted. Eley laments: '*Socialists had lost their confidence in the state*. Without this Archimedean point, their capacity for imagining anti-capitalist alternatives dissolved' (my emphasis).[121] This catches the problem of 'the left' in ways Eley can't quite grasp. What does seem true is that the brand of reformist socialism that always looked to statist solutions, which Marx and Engels criticised in its early manifestations in the 19th century, and whose regular failings Eley himself has documented in his account of the 20th century, is now immensely weakened, as the rival statist 'socialism' associated with Stalinism is also finished.

Eley is inclined to regret their passing. We should not. What Eley regards as the steady undermining of the socialist left over the past third of a century involves several interrelated but partly contradictory developments. What has *not* occurred is a diminution in the *potential strength* of working class organisation, although the undeniable shifts in occupational composition have altered the inner organisational character of the social networks that make up the contemporary working class. Stalinism—a huge impediment to socialist politics all through the extended middle of the 20th century—has been fatally weakened. As for social democracy, while (as Eley remarks) its capacity for regeneration is considerable, the very capitalist success on which it is premised looks more doubtful, and the national-state reformism to which it appeals has been extensively undermined by contemporary developments in world economy.

Looking forward and back

So, finally, where are we now? Not, I think, in the rather depressed environment that Eley offers us as his book ends with a farewell to the 20th century. In the very last days of that century, it was already apparent that rapidly expanding spaces were being opened up, across Europe and the world, for new movements of opposition to both capitalist globalisation and imperialist war-making. If the demonstrations in Seattle at the very end of November 1999 were a brilliant signal of what was to come, the materials to make them had been prepared for several years before. There are indeed plenty of 'reasons to be cheerful'.[122]

The long 'downturn' of working class containment and defeat that followed the upsurge of the 1960s no longer constrains the aspirations and imaginations of new generations in the way it did during the 1980s and much of the 1990s. The space for socialists to spread their ideas has expanded hugely. Terms like 'capitalism' and 'imperialism', which might have seemed part of an antique lexicon only a decade ago, are now part of everyday radical currency. And all the issues in the great debates of the past are now resurfacing: not just utopian ideas but also arguments about whether and how they can be reconciled with practical strategising; serious books on the feasibility of socialist economics are selling well;[123] thousands upon thousands of activists organised the largest demonstration in Britain's entire history in February 2003, against the war on Iraq; it may be that we are no nearer agreement about how, in the words of a famous banner of 2002, to replace capitalism with 'something nicer', but the question itself is very alive, as are wide-ranging questions about the expansion of participatory democracy. Barely commented on, too, because so taken for granted, is the leading role that many young women play in the new anti-capitalist movements, in ways that a previous generation of women might only have dreamed of.

What, in the end, is sad about Eley's history is that, as a product of the dominant political sensibilities of the downturn years, it never prepares the reader for the possibilities that are now erupting around us. If Geoff Eley were to prepare a second edition in a few years' time, I hope he might tell his tale rather differently.

NOTES

1: 'So here I am, in the middle way, having had 20 years—Twenty years largely wasted, the years of l'entre deux guerres'—T S Eliot.

2: G Eley, *Forging Democracy* (Oxford, 2003); see also A Callinicos, 'Bourgeois Revolutions and Historical Materialism', *International Socialism* 43 (Summer 1989), pp113-171.

3: *Forging Democracy*, as above, p10.

4: As above, p4.

5: As above, ppviii-ix. T Shanin draws a similar contrast between periods when 'the alternativity of history' is low, when the dominant images are of repetition and stability, and other periods or 'axial stages' when 'The locks of rigidly determined behaviours, self censored imaginations, and self evident stereotypes of common sense are broken, and the sky seems the limit, or all hell breaks loose.' T Shanin, *Revolution As a Moment of Truth* (London, 1985), p312.

6: *Forging Democracy*, as above, pviii.

7: As above, p8.

8: As above, p20.

9: As above, p21.

10: As above, p27.

11: As above, p78.

12: E J Hobsbawm, 'Custom, Wages and Work-Load in the Nineteenth Century', in *Labouring Men* (London, 1964).

13: *Forging Democracy*, as above, p30.

14: As above, p55.

15: As above, p56.

16: See, for instance, H Draper and A G Lipow, 'Marxist Women and Bourgeois Feminism', *The Socialist Register 1976* (London, 1976).

17: *Forging Democracy*, as above, p14.

18: As above, p23.

19: As above, p22.

20: K Marx and F Engels, *The Germany Ideology*, (London, 1964), p86.

21: K Marx, 'Theses on Feuerbach', in *The German Ideology*, as above, pp645-647.

22: In the same spirit, Marx and Engels look back jointly in 1879 to insist, 'When the International was formed, we expressly formulated the battle-cry: The emancipation of the working class must be the work of the working class itself. We cannot ally ourselves, therefore, with people who openly declare that the workers are too uneducated to free themselves and must therefore be liberated from above by philanthropic big bourgeois and petty bourgeois.' K Marx and F Engels, 'Circular letter to Bebel, Liebknecht, Bracke, et al' (1879) in K Marx, *The First International and After* (Harmondsworth, 1993), p375.

23: H Draper, 'The Two Souls of Socialism', *International Socialism*, first series, 11 (1962), pp12-20. The text has been reproduced in many other places. It can be found on the web at http://www.anu.edu.au/polsci/marx/contemp/pamsetc/twosouls/twosouls.htm

24: *Forging Democracy*, as above, p22.

25: As above, p37.

26: As above, p508.

27: As above, p45.

28: The same recognition was also manifested on the right. Roberto Michels, in his *Political Parties* (first published in 1908), developed the conservative side of the revisionist argument in the direction of total elitist pessimism. The need for organisation, he suggested, always and everywhere generated 'oligarchy', which must itself impede the struggle for socialism. Thus socialism was, through its inner necessities, impossible to achieve. For a critical assessment of Michels' thesis, see C Barker, 'Robert Michels and the Cruel Game', in C Barker, A Johnson and M Lavalette (eds) *Leadership in Social Movements* (Manchester, 2001), pp24-43.

29: *Forging Democracy*, as above, p133.

30: As above, p135.

31: As above, pp144-145.

32: For discussion of these dynamics in five sets of events from the later 20th century, see C Barker (ed), *Revolutionary Rehearsals* (London, 1987).

33: *Forging Democracy*, as above, p141.

34: As above, p146.

35: As above, pp147-148.

36: Eley cites the chilling speech of Moscow financier and industrialist Pavel Riabushinski on 3 August 1917: 'It will take the bony hand of hunger and national destitution to grasp at the throats of these false friends of the people, these members of various committees and soviets, before they will come to their senses', as above, p142.

37: As above, p148.

38: As above, p152.

39: C Harman, 'Gramsci or Eurocommunism?', *International Socialism* 98, first series (May 1977), pp23-26.

40: *Forging Democracy*, as above, p120.

41: As above, p162.

42: As above, p165.

43: As above, p168.

44: As above, p169.

45: As above, p169.

46: See C Harman, *The Lost Revolution: Germany 1918-1923* (London, 1982).

47: *Forging Democracy*, as above, p172.

48: As above, p172.

49: As above, p173.

50: As above, p174.

51: As above.

52: For a fine recent account, see T Behan, *The Resistible Rise of Benito Mussolini* (London, 2003).

53: *Forging Democracy*, as above, p183.

54: See, for example, T Cliff, *Lenin*, volume 1: *Building the Party* (London, 1975).

55: *Forging Democracy*, as above, p184.

56: As above, p179.

57: As above, p222.

58: G Lukács, *A Defence of History and Class Consciousness* (London, 2000), p47.

59: On the containment of even the apparently innocuous Friendly Societies, see S Yeo 'State and Anti-State: Reflections on Social Forms and Struggles from 1850', in P Corrigan (ed), *Capitalism, State Formation and Marxist Theory* (London, 1980), pp111-142.

60: A Shandro, '"Consciousness from Without": Marxism, Lenin and the Proletariat', *Science and Society* 59.3 (1995), pp268-297.

61: As above.

62: In this respect, there is an important difference between the mostly uncritical modern literature on 'new social movements' and Marxism.

63: Marxism was born out of reflection on the already developed achievements and experience of workers' movements in Britain, France, Silesia and elsewhere; Marx and Engels drew their account of 'the dictatorship of the proletariat' from the practices of the Paris Commune; the Bolsheviks learned the significance of soviets from the organisational accomplishments of Russian workers; Marxists (where they were not utterly bone-headed) learned from the women's movements and the gay and lesbian movements of the 1960s and 1970s, etc, etc. If, on the one hand, Lenin insisted that Marxist ideas have to be imported into the spontaneous movement 'from without', key steps in Marxism's own development came to it equally from 'outside' its own ranks.

64: If repeated sequences of events suggest there are organisational patterns to such 'mediating forces', then further theorisation is required. That theorisation may be initially rather vulgar and insufficient. Thus it was with both 'residual petty bourgeoisie' and 'labour aristocracy' theories of the roots of revisionism in the early 20th century. On the former, see for example C Johnson, 'The Problem of Reformism and Marx's Theory of Fetishism', *New Left Review* 119 (January-February 1980), pp70-96. On 'labour aristocracy' theories of reformism, see T Cliff, 'Economic Roots of Reformism', *Socialist Review* (June 1957); reprinted in T Cliff, *Marxist Theory After Trotsky: Selected Writings, vol 3* (London, 2003), pp177-186.

65: G Lukács, as above.

66: *Forging Democracy*, as above, p237.

67: As above, p238.

68: As above, pp238-239.

69: As above. One qualification: the 'hard-wiring' had been largely accomplished well before 1914, as, for example, R Miliband showed long ago in his great *Parliamentary Socialism* (London, 1961), a work unaccountably missing from Eley's references.

70: *Forging Democracy*, as above, p262.

71: As above, p236.

72: As above, p270.

73: As above, p271.

74: None of this implies some necessary vituperativeness on the revolutionary left, as if that is the key thing to learn from Lenin, but it does imply clarity.

75: *Forging Democracy*, as above, p274.

76: As above, p275.

77: As above, p274.

78: Our tendency developed the argument that the post-war long boom was founded on arms spending. See, for example, T Cliff, 'Perspectives for the Permanent War Economy', *Socialist Review* (March 1957), reprinted in T Cliff, *Marxist Theory After Trotsky, Selected Writings, vol 3* (London, 2003), pp169-176; and M Kidron, *Western Capitalism Since the War* (London, 1968).

79: *Forging Democracy*, as above, p288.

80: As above, p297.

81: As above, p296.

82: As above, p296.

83: A MacIntyre, 'Breaking the Chains of Reason', in E P Thompson et al (eds), *Out Of Apathy* (London, 1960), p195.

84: *Forging Democracy*, as above, p348.

85: As above, p350.

86: As above, pp352-353.

87: As above, p414.

88: As above, p399.

89: See, for example, P Foot, *Immigration and Race in British Politics* (Harmondsworth, 1965).

90: *Forging Democracy*, as above, p378.

91: E P Thompson, 'The Peculiarities of the English', *The Socialist Register 1965* (London, 1965), reprinted in E P Thompson, *The Poverty of Theory* (London, 1978).

92: *Forging Democracy*, as above, ch 23.

93: As above, p394.

94: As above.

95: For a critique, see C Barker and G Dale, 'Protest Waves in Western Europe: A Critique of "New Social Movement" Theory', *Critical Sociology* 24.1/2 (1998), pp65-104.

96: *Forging Democracy*, as above, p397.

97: It is a little more fleshed out in C Barker and G Dale, as above. See also for an excellent historical study C Harman, *The Fire Last Time: 1968 and After* (London, 1988).

98: *Forging Democracy*, as above, p389.

99: As above, p391.

100: See, for example, A Callinicos and M Simons, 'The Great Strike; The Miners' Strike of 1984-5 and its Lessons', *International Socialism* 27 (Spring, 1985).

101: For a good discussion of some of the dynamics involved, see R Fantasia and J Stepan-Norris, 'Labor Movement in Motion', in D A Snow, S A Soule and H Kriesi (eds), *The Blackwell Companion to Social Movements* (Oxford, 2004), pp555-575.

102: For good contemporary comment, see T Cliff, 'The Balance of Class Forces in Recent Years' *International Socialism* 6 (Autumn 1979), reprinted in T Cliff, *In the Thick of Workers' Struggle: Selected Writings, vol 2* (London, 2002), pp373-422.

103: *Forging Democracy*, as above, pp401-402.

104: As above, p403.

105: As above, p412.

106: As above. He doesn't mention that this was also the outcome in Britain...

107: As above, p415.

108: As above, p416.

109: As above, pp431-455.

110: As above, pp433-436.

111: As above, p437.

112: As above, pp448-449.

113: See for example, C Barker and C Mooers, 'Theories of Revolution in the Light of 1989 in Eastern Europe', *Cultural Dynamics* 9.1 (1997), pp17-43; L Fuller, *Where Was the Working Class? Revolution in Eastern Germany* (Illinois, 1999) and G Dale, *Popular Protest in East Germany: The Revolution of 1989* (London, 2004).

114: *Forging Democracy*, as above, p450.

115: As above, p451.

116: As above, p457.

117: As above, p583.

118: As above, p481.

119: As above, p482.

120: As above.

121: As above, p483.

122: M Steel, *Reasons to be Cheerful* (London, 2001). A wonderfully funny book.

123: See, for example, M Albert, *Parecon: Life After Capitalism* (London, 2003), A Callinicos, *An Anti-Capitalist Manifesto* (London, 2003).

APOLOGY

Alex Callinicos, Lindsey German and Bookmarks Publications offer their sincere apologies to Quintin Hoare and Branka Magas in connection with a book entitled *The Balkans, Nationalism and Imperialism*.

Mr Hoare is the director of the Bosnian Institute, a UK charity which provides education and information on the history and culture of Bosnia-Herzegovina. Ms Magas is a professional historian who is currently writing a book on the history of Croatia.

In an essay within the book, written by Alex Callinicos, it was stated that the regime of Franjo Tudjman in Croatia, where he was president from 1990, had 'found apologists on the left— for example, Branka Magas and Quintin Hoare. This is surprising since Tudjman is a Holocaust revisionist, the author of a book which claimed that the wartime pro-Nazi Ustashe State in Croatia hadn't killed large numbers of Jews, Serbs and Muslims.'

The allegation that Mr Hoare and Ms Magas had been apologists for the Tudjman regime and/or Franjo Tudjman himself is wholly untrue. Mr Callinicos, Ms German and Bookmarks Publications Ltd have agreed to pay them each a sum by way of damages and their legal costs. They have also undertaken not to repeat the allegation.

The self conscious critic

Rob Hoveman

A review of Terry Eagleton, **After Theory** *(Allen Lane, 2003), £18.99*

Terry Eagleton has produced a highly readable, lucid and amusingly written book, strangely called *After Theory*. Strangely because the book is packed with theories and ideas which tumble out non-stop and at such speed that one would appreciate Eagleton drawing breath and developing the ideas a little more.

The first half of the book is an attempt to draw up a balance sheet of the contribution to the understanding of 'culture' made by the 'cultural theory' of which Eagleton is now professor at Manchester University. For many this may seem a dry and academic exercise in self justification. Presumably cultural theory has its good and its bad bits, and Professor Eagleton is here to rectify the latter and supplement the former. And so in a sense he does, but the result is far from dry and academic even if in the end it is also not entirely satisfactory.

For many it may not be clear what cultural theory is. It can partly be defined by its main theorists: Eagleton includes in his list of the pioneers and greatest theorists of cultural theory Jacques Lacan, Claude Lévi-Strauss, Louis Althusser, Roland Barthes and Michel Foucault. Other names include Raymond Williams, Pierre Bourdieu, Julia Kristeva, Jacques Derrida, Jürgen Habermas, Fredric Jameson and Edward Said.

These and others brought to the study of culture (in its broadest sense) interpretations and applications of Freudian psychoanalysis, structuralism, feminism and semiotics. Eagleton makes some very big claims about their writings. In large part he believes that these theorists were borne aloft by the radicalisation of 1968, that it was with these theorists rather than with the artists, novelists, sculptors and composers that a culturally exciting movement bearing comparison with that between 1910 and 1925 emerged. He further contends that their engagement in a comradely and constructive way with what he calls 'classical' Marxism enabled genuine intellectual progress to take place. This is especially so with the development of feminist theory connected to the women's movement, about which he waxes uncritically.

More specifically, Eagleton claims cultural theory:

…was there to remind the traditional left of what it had flouted: art, pleasure, gender, power, sexuality, language, madness, desire, spirituality, the family, the body, the ecosystem, the unconscious, ethnicity, lifestyle, hegemony. This, on any estimate, was a sizeable slice of human existence.[1]

And yet almost in the next breath he goes on to argue that this was somewhat unjust. Culture had:

…bulked large in the tradition which has come to be known as Western Marxism. Georg Lukács, Walter Benjamin, Antonio Gramsci, Wilhelm Reich, Max Horkheimer, Herbert Marcuse, Theodor Adorno, Ernst Bloch, Lucien Goldmann, Jean-Paul Sartre, Fredric Jameson: these are hardly thinkers who ignored the erotic and symbolic, art and the unconscious, lived experience and transformations of consciousness.[2]

Nor should Marxism be expected to cover, never mind explain, according to Eagleton, every facet of human existence.

Unfortunately Eagleton does not nail the bankruptcy of the official Stalinist Marxism which had dominated the intellectual landscape since the 1930s. And many would rightly take issue with how much cultural theorists genuinely contributed to a general improvement in our understanding of the world, especially if we want to radically change it. Within much of this writing, radical though it seemed in its early stages, lay the seeds of the later developments into postmodernist pessimism and conservatism of which Eagleton is justifiably scathing.

Eagleton believes that the cultural explosion of the late 1960s was displaced into theory because the modernist revolution of the first two decades of the 20th century simply could not repeat itself in the frontline arts. This was partly because repetition is not original and creativity requires originality by definition. Also, the circumstances in which modernism prospered no longer obtained. Modernism was born out of the disintegration of a relatively solid and stable bourgeois world in which all that was solid was melting into air. By the 1960s modernism had been co-opted by the ever-resourceful capitalist order.

But there is an ambivalence here. When Eagleton draws up the balance sheet on cultural theory, he finds largely in its favour, and yet the balance sheet is surprisingly thin on achievements. He frequently nods approvingly in the direction of feminist theory in particular, but provides no lasting paradigms in the book from feminist theory, much less from other elements of the high canon of cultural theory. The writers of Eagleton's canon may have much to be said for them aesthetically and imaginatively, but is it really the case that Barthes or Lacan, for example, have made lasting contributions to our body of knowledge and theory? And when Eagleton does identify the holes in cultural theory, as we will see later, they amount to a pretty big slice of human existence, as Eagleton puts it, which raises questions about why they missed these issues, questions which Eagleton fails to answer.

Eagleton goes on to draw a contrast between the high point of 'high theory', ie the 1970s writings of these theorists, which happens to be the period in which he was most under their collective influence, and the period of decline which followed. He is rightly critical of the intellectual holes in the postmodernist complacency of Fish and Rorty, the recent promoters of American postmodernism.

> For anti-theorists like Richard Rorty and Stanley Fish, theory is how you try to justify your way of life… But this, for anti-theorists, is neither possible or necessary. You cannot justify your way of life by theory because theory is part of that way of life, not something set apart from it… So cultures have no foundation in reason. They just do what they do.[3]

This is a false anti-foundationalism, however, because for the likes of

Rorty and Fish culture has in fact replaced god, nature or reason as the bedrock beneath which we cannot go. However true it may be that there are intellectual limits to how far we can rationally justify or condemn certain deep-seated cultural, social or intellectual practices, political problems become very apparent when we lose sight of the deep-seated compared to the superficial, or have no means for distinguishing between the two. Rorty and Fish have a perspective which lends itself to an ultimately incoherent but also reactionary relativism. From seemingly impeccable and trendy post-modernist principles it can be argued we cannot condemn NATO if we are in one society or female circumcision in another.

Eagleton is keen to justify the attraction of cultural theory to the critical intellectual. In the past such intellectuals, seeking to explore broader questions from the general ordering of society to the meaning of life, would have been attracted to theology before its displacement by science, then by science before it became submerged by specialisation and fragmentation and by philosophy in those traditions where philosophy had not abandoned such aspirations for the dryly technical and frankly trivial.

Cultural theory had the enormous advantage in its early develop-ment of being a subject which crossed traditional academic boundaries. At times Eagleton sounds as though he's been fighting for course reform just a little too long. Cultural theorists also had the good fortune of apparently attracting the radical student seeking an alternative to capitalism's crass careerism and materialism. No figures are given for how many of these stu-dents ended up in investment banks and advertising as opposed to the SWP.

There is also in Eagleton's account an element of the lone intellec-tual as hero holding up her critical corner as all around collapse into postmodernist accommodation. There is of course an element of truth to this. Eagleton has held out as one of the most radical and politically engaged luminaries of British academia. But there should also be a sense of proportion.

In terms of the specific achievements of cultural theory, Eagleton identifies four. First, it has helped to make us self conscious of the process of interpretation, liberating countless English students from the dreary anti-theoretical approach of the liberal humanist tradition that prevailed in so much literature teaching at least into the 1970s. Cultural theory is then the coming to self consciousness and to self criticism of criticism itself.

Second, it has shown us that there is not just one correct way to understand, for example, a work of fiction. Thus *Wuthering Heights* can be seen both as a novel about death and about the Freudian death drive, and Jane Austen as an author who deals with love, marriage and moral values, and someone who consciously or otherwise relates these crucially to property and social class. To see cultural works as open to more than one interpretation is not to become a meaning nihilist and see them as open to any interpretation. But it is to free us from the tyranny of the one-dimensional.

True as this is, the multiple but nonetheless limited number of interpretations available are surely not just a matter of aesthetic choice, as Eagleton almost seems to imply. It would be reductionist simply to provide an interpretation of Austen which talked of class and property, but it is to miss something essential in any understanding of Austen if you don't bring in class and property. On the other hand, I am much more dubious about the virtues of discerning the Freudian death drive in *Wuthering Heights*, because, fascinating though the theory is, I am much more dubious about its truth.

Third, it has helped us to see cultural works as the product of more than the author's conscious intentions. The work has to be understood in its totality, which includes the unconscious, the context and the reader's contribution, something Eagleton is keen to emphasise.

Fourth, there is the link between culture and power. This runs against the liberal and conservative view that culture is the very opposite of power, indeed a haven free from power's unlovely sway. Eagleton acknowledges that 'culture has acted as a precious remembrance of utopia'.[4] And yet culture can also be complicit with unsavoury forms of power. 'Indeed, these two aspects of culture are not unrelated. By encouraging us to dream beyond the present, it may also provide the existing social order with a convenient safety valve'.[5]

Eagleton's balance sheet on cultural theory is broadly favourable. He accepts that some of its practitioners have written in an extremely bad style and with dubious meaning. But its high theorists have largely been great writers as well as thinkers. He defends writing clearly, and as a master stylist himself, puts that into practice. But he also defends the view that just because culture is something shared in the way that astrophysics is not, it does not mean that understanding culture should not be fraught with difficult ideas and at times technical language.

If much of the criticism that has been levelled at cultural theory has been 'either false or fairly trifling', according to Eagleton:

> ...a far more devastating criticism of it can be launched. Cultural theory as
> we have it promises to grapple with some fundamental problems, but on the
> whole fails to deliver. It has been shamefaced about morality and meta-
> physics, embarrassed about love, biology, religion and revolution, largely
> silent about evil, reticent about death and suffering, dogmatic about essences,
> universals and foundations, and superficial about truth, objectivity and disin-
> terestedness. This, on any estimate, is rather a large slice of human existence
> to fall down on.[6]

From Chapter 5 onwards Eagleton moves out of a rather narrow and
academic debate into much more ambitious territory. He gives two reasons
why cultural theory must now address the big issues. First, he believes that
the challenge to the West from 'Islamic fundamentalism' will inevitably
force Western intellectuals to address the broader questions of legitimation
of the Western order in one form or another. In other words the 'end of
history' thesis that Western liberal capitalism had finally triumphed went
hand in hand with the postmodern rejection (ironically) of 'grand narratives', with emphasis on the particular rather than the general, on difference
rather than the universal, etc. The end of history is clearly not nigh with
the advent of Islamic fundamentalism, therefore we need to address the big
issues cultural theory has been earnestly avoiding.

More pertinent are the very favourable but very abstract references
Eagleton makes to the emergence of the anti-capitalist movement. But even
here he is woolly. Eagleton claims in an extraordinary couple of sentences
that 'there can be no falling back on ideas of collectivity which belong to a
world unravelling before our eyes. Human history is for the most part both
post-collectivist and post-individualist'.[7] In case we should despair at this
early point in the book he goes on: 'We need to imagine new forms of
belonging, which in our kind of world are bound to be multiple rather than
monolithic... The anti-capitalist movement is seeking to sketch out new
relations between globality and locality, diversity and solidarity'.[8]

This is somewhat typical. Eagleton has always had his heart on the left
and his roots in the Marxist tradition. He has had more connection than
some left academics with real political activity. I remember him selling *Big
Flame* outside the King's Arms in Oxford in the late 1970s and spending a

couple of hours on the coldest day of winter collecting in Oxford's Cornmarket for the miners in 1984. He frequently talks favourably in his books, his lectures and his seminars of the one and only successful workers' revolution in Russia in October 1917, and this book is no exception. His sympathies and his values are those of the Marxist intellectual.

But he has also spent many years immersed in academia, reading, writing and lecturing voraciously. His Marxism owes much to the orthodox Trotskyist tradition from which weaknesses in his analysis of the Soviet Union and its fall originate. He certainly used to believe that the fall of the Berlin Wall in 1989 bore out Trotsky's view, articulated in the 1930s, and faithfully preserved for the following 50 years by Ernest Mandel, that the Soviet Union was indeed a degenerated workers' state which was like an inverted pyramid balancing precariously and finally toppling over. The weaknesses in that tradition come through occasionally in his willingness to accept Maoism and even apparently the state ideology of Stalinism as part of the Marxist tradition. And although it can be crass to seek to exclude from the canon anyone who doesn't agree with the tradition narrowly defined, too much liberalism fails to provide the necessary analytical tools to draw the line. That may be partly why he is so generous to those who have abandoned the Marxist tradition, acknowledging this move only very late in their trajectory away from 'comradely' engagement with Marxism.

He has also long been fascinated by theorists and theories with at best a tenuous connection with the classical Marxist tradition. He certainly seems a little out of touch with the political realities of the contemporary world. It seems odd to write off 'old forms' of collective identity just because the defeats of the last 20 years have put the working class on the defensive. Eagleton makes no attempt to justify the view that there has been a fundamental change in the structure of society to undermine the classical Marxist view of the proletariat as the potential gravediggers of capitalism. He just seems to take it as obvious. Yet the upsurge of struggles in France in 1995 and again this year show that the working class can begin to re-emerge from the dark night of defeat and downturn, just as the re-emergence of the unofficial wildcat strike has done in Britain.

His positive view of the anti-capitalist movement is presented at such a lofty level of abstraction it is difficult to know what to make of his view of its potential. He certainly shows no awareness of the different views now prevalent within and dividing the anti-capitalist movement.

Nonetheless, there is still plenty of justification for properly addressing the deep philosophical issues which preoccupy Eagleton in the second half of the book. There is much confusion about the nature of truth and morality in areas of academia—including in particular those areas affected most by (formerly) trendy but generally poor philosophy emanating from France and the US (as well as having its home-grown varieties).

Eagleton is quite right to lambast relativism about truth, which ultimately implodes in its own inconsistencies. He does a service in carefully showing that believing in 'absolute' truth is not to believe in dogma, or revealed truth. It is simply to believe in a concept of truth which avoids inconsistency and logical self contradiction, a minimum requirement for rational thought and dialogue. This does not make the truth easy to obtain or our claims to truth unfalsifiable. On the contrary, it is the relativist who has a concept of truth more compatible with dogmatism. While there has been some confusion about the concept of truth in the classical Marxist tradition, what Eagleton has to say about truth seems to me to be compatible with the best of that tradition and to have the virtue of being true.

Similarly, Eagleton outlines clearly and cogently a concept of human nature which provides a value concept of self realisation. This would be rejected by all those 'anti-essentialist' postmodernists, but again on spurious and ultimately incoherent philosophical grounds. This concept of human nature, itself complex and contested, is to be found in Aristotle and, socialised, underpins Marx's concept of human nature. More than that, Eagleton outlines a concept of morality rooted in that concept of human nature and human potential which underpins Marx's critique of capitalism. Again there has been some confusion on this question within the tradition, but Eagleton seems to me correct in seeing the problem as arising from the failure to distinguish between moralism and morality:

> For Aristotle…ethics and politics are intimately related. Ethics is about excelling at being human, and nobody can do this in isolation. Moreover, nobody can do it unless the political institutions which allow you to do it are available. It is this kind of moral thinking which was inherited by Karl Marx… Questions of good and bad had been falsely abstracted from their social contexts, and had to be restored to them again. In this sense, Marx was a moralist in the classical sense of the word. He believed that moral enquiry had to examine all of the factors which went to make up a specific action or way of life, not just personal ones.[9]

Marx, however, thought that, on the whole, 'morality' was ideology, argues Eagleton, because he confused morality with moralism, where moralism is the view that 'there is a set of questions known as moral questions which are quite distinct from social or political ones'.[10]

The arguments and ideas in the second half of the book are original, dense and stimulating. They include not only serious thinking on questions of truth, objectivity and value but also on the meaning of death and its implications for life, an attempt to penetrate 'fundamentalist' thinking, and a radical anti-fundamentalist and anti-dogmatic interpretation of the moral understanding Eagleton believes to be present in parts of the Christian Bible.

While Eagleton is good at exposing the limitations of the views he is opposed to, and often compelling on the views that he favours, he does not always go very deeply into the philosophical issues and does not answer or address some of the very hard questions, at least in adequate detail. Indeed Eagleton might accept that his brilliant *tour de force* in the second half of the book is more a prologue to a much more substantial, essentially philosophical, theory.

One motivation for trying to develop such theory is the re-emergence of essentially familiar philosophical problems in postmodernism and their use to undermine rather than strengthen movements to challenge capitalist barbarism. Eagleton seems to feel postmodernism has pretty much had its day, but that fundamentalism now provides the motivation to think seriously about fundamental issues. Certainly there is useful work to be done in clarifying and strengthening the philosophical underpinnings of our theory of working class self emancipation. It seems to me Eagleton has made a very useful contribution to that project in the second half of this book.

NOTES

1: T Eagleton, *After Theory* (Harmondsworth, 2003), p30.

2: As above.

3: As above, p54.

4: As above, p90.

5: As above, p100.

6: As above, pp101-102.

7: As above, p21.

8: As above, pp21-22.

9: As above, p143.

10: As above.

All praise the market!

Phil Marfleet

A review of Nigel Harris, **The Return of Cosmopolitan Capital: Globalisation, the State and War** *(IB Tauris, 2003),* £24.50

I read this book with a sense of increasing scepticism, becoming incredulity. By the end I also felt indignation that the author could claim to address 'the old agenda of socialists' while advancing theories of economic and political change which sit comfortably with those of the most aggressive neo-liberals. *The Return of Cosmopolitan Capital* is less a book about capitalism than an apology for it, in particular for the ravages of globalisation.

Nigel Harris has always written books crammed with information. This one too contains a mass of data of real interest, especially on the world economy before the coming of industrial capitalism. But this material is incidental to the main plot—Harris's account of the changing relationship between the state and capital. Developing an argument he began to set out in the early 1990s[1] he suggests that for the past 500 years the most important feature of world history has been a continuing struggle between merchants and traders—the 'cosmopolitan bourgeoisie'—and those who operate territorial states. The kings, princes and politicians who dominated states, says Harris, succeeded in subordinating world trade networks to local control, inhibiting and distorting the positive features of capitalist development. They misdirected productive resources into war—hence Harris's concern is with 'the war-making state', with its waste and destructive power.

Much of the book is a detailed account of successive phases of the struggle between commercial capital—seeking to move freely across the globe—and the efforts of local states to compel the market to serve their own ends. The war-making state is malign, argues Harris, and it is only when its influence is diminished that the potentials of capitalism can be realised. Globalisation, he maintains, is now driving the state into retreat; in effect the era of states and of war-making is reaching its end and the productive capacity of capital—that is, capital as trade—can initiate a new period of global well being.

Harris foresees 'a new bourgeois revolution'—'the establishment of the power of world markets and of businessmen over the states of the world'.[2] It is this that will serve the interests of the mass of humanity, ending poverty and making 'the conditions of all consistent with the best'.[3] The more there is of uninhibited capitalism the more there will be prosperity and harmony; the 'return' of the bourgeoisie, released at last from the tyranny of the state, will mark the moment of advance of the many.

Super-globaliser

The key contention here—that extension of the market brings universal good—is awfully familiar. It can be seen in almost any strategic document produced by the major transnational financial institutions. In its report on the world economy, *Entering the 21st Century*, the World Bank, for example, insists that full engagement with world commerce is a requirement for the countries of Africa, Asia and Latin America. According to the World Bank, 'For developing countries, trade is the primary vehicle for realising the benefits of globalisation'.[4] Like the World Bank, the International Monetary Fund (IMF) and the World Trade Organisation (WTO), Harris believes that embracing the world market is the key to economic and social advance. He is not just a globaliser, however, but a super-globaliser. In common with pioneers of globalist theory such as Kenichi Ohmae he maintains that states abuse the productive capacities of capitalism. Ohmae argues that 'the nation-state has become an unnatural, even dysfunctional unit for organising human activity and managing economic endeavour in a borderless world'.[5] But Harris believes that the state has *always* been 'dysfunctional' and that only when global capital has reconquered the world of states can we look forward to an era of prosperity and harmony.

Harris sees the state as an incubus, an alien force that for centuries has haunted the bourgeoisie, seizing and redirecting all the potentials of commerce for its own interests. But the relationship between capital and the state is far more complex than is suggested by this struggle between good and evil. Since the emergence of the nation-state it has been impossible to dissociate the state as such from capital and from the agendas of capitalists. To be sure, at various phases of capitalist development governments have accommodated or strongly encouraged the commercial and industrial bourgeoisies, while during other periods they have restricted them. States have often been strongly identified with private capital, while some dominated by the bureaucracy and the military have set out to regulate capital in their own interests, hence state capitalism. Even in this context, however, it is wrong to see the state merely as an independent category, a political actor in its own right. States have a class character—they are dominated by men and women who have specific interests vis-à-vis the mass of the population and who mobilise resources to maintain their positions of privilege. When the formal structure of the state changes, as in a revolutionary upheaval, there may be a change in power relations to the disadvantage of capitalists. In other cases, however, as with recent developments in the former Soviet Union, many of those who formerly enjoyed power have been able to retain positions of privilege. The key issue is the actuality of class relationships.

Much of Nigel Harris's work in the 1960s and 1970s focused directly on this issue. His analysis of Mao's China, *The Mandate of Heaven*, was a corrective to the approach of those who saw the Chinese state as a new model of popular power.[6] At a time when many on the left were seduced by the rhetoric of China's rulers—by the idea of peasant uprisings, military means to power, and 'cultural revolution'—Harris examined the reality of class relationships, concluding that a new bureaucratic state capitalism had emerged. Curiously, *Cosmopolitan Capital* contains no reference to *The Mandate of Heaven*, not even in a bibliography which lists many of Harris's publications. Not does it undertake any analysis of class relations within a state or specific states; rather it assumes 'the war-making state' as an undifferentiated category which is pitched in constant struggle against capital. How shallow this approach is when compared to Harris's earlier insights.

Drive to war

At several points in *Cosmopolitan Capital* Harris is at pains to point out the shortcomings of the Marxist perspective. Marx, he says, was 'beguiled', 'wrong', 'misguided'—indeed Marx and Marxists appear so often in the text that one begins to feel that the author protests too much.[7] But despite his ambitious project—to provide a world history of relations between the state and capital—nowhere does he suggest a alternative to the Marxist perspective as a whole.

This is especially striking in relation to processes of change, notably the crucial issue of the rise of industrial capitalism. Harris asserts that this system emerged because those who controlled the early centralised states of Europe wished for enhanced means to wage war. They therefore directed local representatives of commercial capital to use their resources for production of *materiel*: 'The heart of the national industrial system was the making of arms and naval vessels, what ultimately became heavy industry'.[8] Long periods of 'manipulation' of private business by the state consolidated industrial production and the special groups of capitalists who were organised to sustain it.[9] Industry, then, was the outcome of the imposition upon merchants and traders—Harris's true capitalists—of priorities dictated by the state's drive to war. This is Harris's challenge to Marx, to the idea that capitalism grew organically within primarily agrarian societies and that this process produced social and political upheavals which were eventually settled in the interests of a new bourgeoisie. Harris enquires rhetorically, 'Was there then no "bourgeois revolution"?'—and answers in the negative.[10]

Harris's method is to pile up data on production for war and to argue by assertion. The thousands of pikes, swords, muskets, cannon, ships, lengths of rope, sail, chain, etc demanded by Europe's princes to wage war on their rivals amount to evidence that the rise of industry was driven by the monarchical state. Harris ignores those who have examined other more fundamental processes at work within European society in the 16th, 17th and 18th centuries. He has nothing to say on changes in class relations within agrarian society. He is silent on the growing impact of merchant capital, the spread of craft industry, and the consolidation of urban-based production—here he might have addressed the insights of Braudel, for example. What of the political upheavals associated with these changes, notably the English and French revolutions? The former hardly makes an appearance except as illustrative material for the war-making thesis—the New Model Army is a passing example of a novel type of military formation.[11] Events in France are described simply as 'a monster of popular nationalism'.[12] Harris ignores the participants in these epoch-making movements. They are simply irrelevant: what is important is the volume of gunpowder, the number of wagons, the tonnage of vessels required to support an escalating drive to war. Harris has removed entirely the men and women who make history.

Nation-states

In the Harris account the state is foisted upon the commercial bourgeoisie. It is the state which misdirects the positive energies of merchant capital, which indeed corrupts trade, destroying the harmonious relations it has generated worldwide. As late as the mid 19th century, he suggests, commercial capital held out the promise of a world integrated by the market: 'Cosmopolitanism seemed to promise a world without nationalism, provincialism and racism, a world in which trade harmonised all'.[13]

On this view commercial capital has an unblemished record. It is innocent of any active engagement with the state. To sustain this idea Harris must again ignore the mass of literature which addresses social and political change in Europe over some 400 years. There are no peasant revolts, urban uprisings, movements for reform, revolutionary crises—certainly none which engage the merchant classes. History—as in the schoolbooks of an earlier era—is the work of princes, kings and emperors. Like the rest of the population, the commercial bourgeoisie is passive and credulous.

Consider the comments by Hill on the character of merchant capital in England:

> By the 17th century some merchants were as rich as peers, though their fortunes were usually made in one lifetime. Such men were quite independent of all but the government. They were busy breaking down the privileges of local corporations where these impeded; and they were using their wealth to reconstruct the society in which they lived.[14]

These men, and the lesser merchants and artisans, played a key role in the English Revolution of the 1640s. They were active in prolonged struggles against the Crown and in years of debate about representation and legitimate authority. To paraphrase E P Thompson, they were present at the making of the modern English state. They were less coerced or 'manipulated' by the state than instrumental in shaping it.

The merchant class was not composed of innocents. It contested both the old order and those movements from below which wished for more radical outcomes—for example, it facilitated the deportation of Leveller activists and later of Irish Republicans and dissenters who refused to take an oath of allegiance to the new state.[15] Eric Williams notes that as a result of mass deportation the island of Monserrat in the Caribbean—a mercantile enterprise—'became largely an Irish colony'.[16]

There was a similar story during the revolutionary events in France. Merchant capital was deeply engaged in constructing the new order. It had blood on its hands—not only that of Louis and his supporters but of the radical activists who demanded more rights than the bourgeoisie was prepared to accommodate. The Republic, which was to have a profound influence on national movements throughout the 19th century, was unthinkable without the engagement of the merchant class. Like all capitalists they required both an apparatus of state and an ideology of belonging which could assist in the struggle to unite inherently unstable populations. They were architects of the nation-state, the particular formation which has served capitalism so well.

Slavery

For Harris it is the world-embracing activity of commercial capital which is so distinctive. This, he argues, has been pursued without the involvement of vulgar political constructions such as the state. Such a view cannot be sustained.

Marx was the first to identify the relationship between colonisation and the world market:

> The discovery of gold and silver in America, the extirpation, enslavement and entombment in mines of the aboriginal population, the beginning of the conquest and looting of the East Indies, the turning of Africa into a warren for the commercial hunting of black skins, signalled the rosy dawn of the era of capitalist production. These idyllic proceedings are the chief moments of primitive accumulation.[17]

The first colonies were constructed upon slave labour. This was indeed driven by the market, by the activities of commercial capital, but it required more than an economic impulse. As Gai observes, the merchants, traders, slavers and plantation owners needed 'the politicisation of space—an organised community, legislation of the use of force, rules, adjudication, and ideology'.[18] The colonising powers developed elaborate codes of ownership and means of regulating disputes among traders and slave-owners. Core structures of the state which had emerged in Europe—legal systems, judicial institutions and means of enforcement—were reproduced in the colonies as mechanisms which both guaranteed the rights of owners of property and mediated relations among them.[19] Here the colonial enterprise was under-written by states in which the merchant class had a stake of its own.

The ruling families of Europe struggled to maintain control of the monarchical state—and most eventually lost. They were also forced to surrender their early colonial possessions. The states which emerged reflected above all the interests and ambitions of commercial capital. Many of the wealthiest people in Britain's American colonies were slave-owners or were closely associated with the trade, among them leading activists of the independence movement. Samuel Johnson, a strong opponent of slavery, observed, 'How is it that we hear the loudest yelps for liberty among the drivers of negroes?'[20]

The American traders and planters demanded a state adequate to their specific needs. Blackburn comments that, 'the most prominent champions [of the American Revolution] included slaveholders and carrying-trade merchants who looked forward to an unfettered advance of the North American involvement in plantation agriculture'.[21] By the mid 19th century similar movements had broken up the Spanish and Portuguese empires in Latin America—in less than 100 years power relations across the Americas changed comprehensively, leaving local merchant capital in an influential position. Rather than being overwhelmed by an abstract, disembodied state, the real individuals who made up the trading networks had engaged in flesh and blood struggles which brought into being new national states which they hoped would better serve their own interests.

'Buccaneers'

By the late 19th century the US and most European governments were attempting to regulate commercial capital much more closely. Even at this stage, however, merchant adventurers played a leading role in their own right. In an earlier era they had been the active element in what Kiernan calls 'private enterprise imperialism', whereby the state endorsed organisations such as the various East India Companies.[22] During the 1870s and

1880s such activities were resumed in Southern Africa, West Africa and China. In 1889 the British South Africa Company was chartered, headed by the profiteer Cecil Rhodes. He made vast sums from gold and diamonds, using much of his fortune to finance land grabs which the British authorities were pleased to endorse. When he created the colony of Rhodesia Europeans flooded in—traders, speculators, carpet-baggers and 'buccaneers'.[23] Similar operations were conducted across the continent—there was a British East Africa Company, a Royal Niger Company, a Deutsche Ostafrikanische Gesellschaft. Their pioneering activities were invariably associated with the drawing of new colonial boundaries and the establishment of new states.

It was not clear, comments Porter, whether the state was 'the tool of mammon' or the capitalists served imperial interest, but in many places diplomats and capitalists 'were found suspiciously together'.[24] This observation sums up neatly the continuing relationship between senior state functionaries and private capitalists in general.

World war and recession

Why did the states of Europe launch the catastrophic wars of the 20th century? For Harris they are the product of state structures themselves: 'War was the very *raison d'être* of the nation, the sacred affirmation of its existence and superiority, its historical validation, beyond all calculations of accident, let alone profit and loss'.[25]

World wars were fought, Harris insists, because states were bound to fight them. He is uninterested in precipitating factors, including the specific conjuncture of global rivalries and the domestic problems of European governments. More important is the industrial character of the conflict: the number of artillery pieces produced, shells fired, aircraft manufactured, vessels launched, men slaughtered. In the case of the Second World War Harris is concerned above all with the construction of the war economy—the activities of states which declared for autarkic strategies in which 'the government made itself supreme', bringing business as a whole under close control and preparing for new conflicts.[26] This is perhaps the most startling section of *Cosmopolitan Capital*, for the drive to war takes place as if the greatest crisis in capitalist history was merely incidental. The Great Depression appears as an extrinsic factor, and the events of the 1920s and 1930s which preceded and accompanied it—including revolutionary turmoil across Europe—have no place in the story.

Harris does go to pains to examine the rise of fascism—or at least one aspect of it. He is concerned to demonstrate that in Germany the Nazis held no brief for big business. They were not a party of capitalism; rather they were the ultimate creation of the war-making state. He looks in detail at relations between Hitler and the barons of German industry and concludes that 'business was reduced to being an instrument of the state, not at all the reverse'.[27] The precise relationship between the Nazi Party and business is a matter of debate, but what is not at issue, surely, is that fascism was a violent opponent of independent mass struggles. Its mission was to bring order to a system in profound crisis—to destroy workers' movements in evidence across Europe and especially assertive in Germany. Reflecting the anxieties of capitalism in general—above all of the fearful small capitalists—it waged war against the movement from below. The 'war-making state' was in this sense a state that struggled to preserve capitalism by liquidating its most potent enemies.

Globalisation

It is with a sense of relief that Harris reaches the calm waters of the post-war era. He notes the long boom of the 1950s and 1960s, which 'lifted almost all the boats, transforming the living conditions, the style of life and the psychologies of millions of people'.[28] If only such growth could be resumed, he suggests, all would benefit.

For Harris globalisation offers this very possibility. Over the past 30 years, he proposes, capital has defied the best efforts of states to continue regulation. New networks of exchange have eroded national boundaries, bringing together physically distant regions, promoting new efficiencies and seeding prosperity across the continents. The agent of this transformation is trade: 'inexorably world markets, step by step, are adjusting political behaviour and responses, creating, all unseen, a new world order'.[29]

If only governments would understand. Their participation could speed progress, serving the interests of all. But many, Harris suggests, are stuck in the past. They continue to see the state as a means to personal advance and influence, they are mere 'rent-seekers' clinging on to power at the cost of the majority.[30] Third World governments unable to reform bear responsibility for the consequences. The crisis in Africa, for example, is an outcome of the failure of its rulers to allow the market to dictate the pace of change. Here regimes were 'too late to change and so unwilling to abandon the national capital project'.[31] Africa could have learned from market-led policies in other parts of the world; instead its people are saddled with corruption and with rulers who may be no more than 'military mafia'.[32]

Harris is shameless. He writes off centuries of ruthless exploitation of sub-Saharan Africa—not just slavery, European settlement, and the colonial state, but generations of one-dimensional 'development' which have produced vulnerable monocultural economies. The role of the latter has in fact been to satisfy the demands of commercial capital—the heroic figures of Harris's world narrative. To assure the flow from Africa of coffee, cocoa, cotton, copper, diamonds and much more, Western governments have endorsed regimes prepared to do their bidding. They have bought up a whole generation of rulers, or where this has proved difficult, created them. The rivalries built into colonial states have been exploited to ensure instability—arms have poured in and all the while crops and minerals vital to production in distant parts of the world have flowed out. The great trading multinationals have made merry while hundreds of millions of people have been pushed to the margin of survival—or beyond.

On his account transnational institutions which have led the offensive are not guilty. Their agendas, says Harris, have had no impact on a process 'driven by markets'.[33] At this point one feels that Harris is commenting on events in another galaxy: is he unaware of the pressures exerted on governments which baulk at Structural Adjustment Programmes (SAPs)? Is there no relationship between arms deliveries to Third World rulers and the latter's willingness to crush opposition to IMF reforms?

Harris ploughs on, blaming the Third World in general and Africa in particular for an inability to change. This *is* the Washington consensus—the view that attributes failures of development to an imperfect alignment with the world market, the task being to neutralise or remove recalcitrant elements, drive back the state and open local economies to the proper disciplines of competition. It is difficult to see what separates Harris from the strategists of the World Bank, the IMF or the WTO. For several years he has worked as a World Bank consultant: does this account for his attachment to their ghastly creed?

Riots

Harris writes as if resistance to market-led policies has been restricted to unco-operative governments—local 'mafia'. He has not noticed that since the IMF introduced its first SAP in the mid-1970s, there have been hundreds of mass protests involving hundreds of millions of people. According to Walton and Seddon, between 1976 and 1992 alone there were almost 150 such events—by the 1980s they had become so common they were routinely described as 'IMF riots'.[34] Many forced governments and the IMF into retreat—to reinstate food subsidies, fixed prices or emergency food stocks. Were the participants simply perverse: should they have accepted the discipline of the market and paid the higher prices? Should they have starved?

Harris likewise ignores the emergence of the anti-capitalist and anti-globalisation movements. His sole reference to the phenomenon is to compare the protesters of Seattle with J M Keynes. Neither, he comments, wished to be at the mercy of world markets; both have pursued the illusion that states can intervene to ameliorate their effects on the mass of people.[35] The collective has no role in bringing change; rather we must place our faith in new bodies which have appeared in the wake of the retreating state—non-governmental organisations (NGOs). They constitute 'all that is left of a fundamental critique of modern society, but also the beginning of a global political forum that reaches well beyond the conventional circle of world power and influence'.[36] Some NGOs do express democratic sentiments—but most do not and are indeed part of the problem.

Harris closes his book with another appeal to the liberating powers of capital. The 'real bourgeois revolution' is on its way, he intones. Echoing Adam Smith he promises that 'the unknown—and unintended—outcome of market transactions' is to be the guarantee of universal well-being.[37] The evidence is already with us: war, Harris says, is a thing of the past and only minor local conflicts remain to be resolved. Oh dear!—has he noticed those little problems in Afghanistan, in Iraq, and the promises of conflicts in Syria, Iran, Korea? The state appears to be fighting fit—and fighting for profit, clearing the way in Iraq for Bechtel, Halliburton and Exxon. As before, politicians and capitalists are 'found suspiciously together'. It is the same old imperialism.

Unlike Harris vast numbers of people worldwide believe that the world is a *more* dangerous place—and fortunately they are prepared to do something about it.

NOTES

1: See N Harris, *National Liberation* (London, 1990), and Harris's contribution to an exchange with Chris Harman and Alex Callinicos in *International Socialism* 51, 53 and 54: 'A Comment on National Liberation', *International Socialism* 53 (Winter 1991).

2: N Harris, *The Return of Cosmopolitan Capital* (London, 2003), p264.

3: As above.

4: *World Bank Development Report* (New York, 2000), p5.

5: K Ohmae, *The End of the Nation State* (London, 1995),p78.

6: N Harris, *The Mandate of Heaven: Marx and Mao in Modern China* (London, 1978).

7: Harris's work still shows the influence of the Marxist perspective within which he produced his early work. Unexplained references to combined and uneven development and to state capitalism may puzzle readers of *Cosmopolitan Capital* who are unfamiliar with the work of Leon Trotsky and of Tony Cliff.

8: N Harris, *Cosmopolitan Capital*, as above, p58.

9: As above, p88.

10: As above, p89.

11: As above, p70.

12: As above, p71.

13: As above, p86. Can Harris really mean that the merchant capitalists of the Atlantic slave trade and those who plundered India and later Africa were making 'a world without nationalism...and racism'—a world of harmony? They were in fact leading actors in constructing racism, inexplicable without the colonial experience in general and that of enslavement in particular.

14: C Hill, *Reformation to Industrial Revolution* (London, 1969), p53.

15: As above, p164.

16: E Williams, *Capitalism and Slavery* (London, 1964), p13.

17: K Marx, *Capital*, Vol I (London, 1954), p703.

18: Y Gai, 'Migrants Workers, Markets and the Law' in W Gunguru (ed), *Global History and Migrations* (Boulder, 1997), p145.

19: See R S Dunn, *Sugar and Slaves* (New York, 1973) for a detailed account of slaving and colonial states in the Caribbean.

20: H Thomas, *The Slave Trade* (London, 1997) p476.

21: R Blackburn, *The Making of New World Slavery* (London, 1995), p472.

22: V G Kiernan, *Colonial Empires and Armies 1815-1960* (London, 1982), p98.

23: B Porter, *The Lion's Share* (London, 1975), p149.

24: As above.

25: N Harris, *The Return of Cosmopolitan Capital*, as above, p78.

26: As above, p96.

27: As above, p114.

28: As above, p129.

29: As above, p219.

30: As above, p164.

31: As above, p166.

32: As above, p168.

33: As above, p170.

34: J Walton and D Seddon, *Free Markets and Food Riots* (Oxford, 1994), pp39-40.

35: N Harris, *The Return of Cosmopolitan Capital*, as above, p97.

36: As above, p248.

37: As above, p264.

The Jubilee and the Apocalypse: a reply

Neil Faulkner

In 'The Jubilee and the Apocalypse' (*International Socialism* 98), John Rose wrote a strong critique of my book *Apocalypse: The Great Jewish Revolt Against Rome, AD 66-73*.[1] The debate is important for two reasons. First, it concerns a crucial stage in the development of the Judaeo-Christian tradition, which, as John points out, has been central to 'Western civilisation'. Second, at a time when US imperialism is a major global issue, it concerns the nature of imperialism in antiquity and the class struggle waged against it. This debate therefore has contemporary resonance. There seem to be four main areas of disagreement, and I shall deal with each in turn.

Historical method

John accuses me of not following the example of Geoffrey de Ste Croix and (a) having a full 'scholarly apparatus', and (b) avoiding the use of 'modern analytical concepts'.[2] The first point is invalid because it amounts to criticising me for not writing a different book. *Apocalypse* is a popular narrative for the general reader, not an academic tome like *The Class Struggle in the Ancient Greek World*. My discussions of source criticism, methodological problems and scholarly debate are therefore restricted to short summaries—whereas they are the very essence of de Ste Croix's work. John's comparison is therefore pointless.

Much more important is his second point. This is worth quoting in full:

...there is his [de Ste Croix's] stern warning about importing modern analytical concepts into ancient-historical analysis. His test was simple. Did the ancient Greeks have a similar concept? If not, then, he writes, 'it may be a salutary warning to us that the phenomenon we are looking at may not have existed'.[3]

Now if de Ste Croix had really meant as John says, then he would have been wrong—wrong in general, wrong about his own method, and wrong in relation to many other statements in the very book from which the quotation is taken. The essence of *The Class Struggle in the Ancient Greek World* is the application of Marxist class analysis to the understanding of ancient history.[4] Let me spell out the obvious in relation to this. No ancient Greek was a Marxist. No ancient Greek had a developed class analysis of history. No ancient Greek could have done because the material basis for such an understanding did not exist in antiquity. Marxism—the theory of international proletarian revolution—could not exist until a class had arisen that contained within itself the possibility of general human emancipation.[5] You cannot have Marxism without the proletariat. That is why Marxism is a product of the 19th century. Up until that moment, all theories of history were tied in some sense to social classes with particular interests; they were, if you like, ideological. A theory of history that was scientific only became possible when a class appeared that had, instead of particular interests, universal ones. We now use that scientific theory to analyse history as a whole, and it is de Ste Croix's great achievement that he pioneered its application to classical antiquity. To argue that we should use only ancient concepts to explain ancient society—to argue, in effect, that ancient society explained itself—is to deny the scientific breakthrough that Marxism represents. In fact, with its implicit denial of any truth beyond a society's own perceptions of itself, it amounts to a collapse into postmodernism. And de Ste Croix was far too good a Marxist to make such a mistake. Here is some more of the passage from which John quoted so selectively:

I feel much happier, in dealing with the history of the ancient Greek world, if I can legitimately make use of categories of social analysis which are not only precise, in the sense that I can define them, but also general, in the sense that they can be applied to the analysis of other human societies. Class, in my sense, is eminently such a category. Nevertheless, I realise that it is a healthy instinct on the part of historians in the empirical tradition to feel the need at

least to *begin from* [de Ste Croix's emphasis] the categories and even the terminology in use within the society they are studying—*provided, of course, they
do not remain imprisoned therein* [my emphasis].[6]

My conclusions may be mistaken in *Apocalypse*, but my historical
method—the use of 'modern analytical concepts' to explain antiquity—
most certainly is not.

Ancient nationalism

John takes particular exception to my use of two modern concepts: nationalism and racism.[7] He disagrees that they are applicable to antiquity, and
takes me to task for not defining what I mean by them. I will take them in
turn, starting in each case with a definition.

John is right to praise Eric Hobsbawm's work on modern nationalism.
He has done as thorough a hatchet job as one could hope for, exposing
nationalist ideologies as fabrications based on invented traditions rooted in
the state-building projects of modern capitalist and proto-capitalist ruling
classes.[8] So let us use Hobsbawm's definition:

> I use the term 'nationalism' in the sense defined by Gellner, namely to mean
> 'primarily a principle which holds that the political and national unit should
> be congruent'. I would add that this principle also implies that the political
> duty of Ruritanians to the polity which encompasses and represents the
> Ruritanian nation, overrides all other public obligations, and in extreme
> cases (such as wars) all other obligations of whatever kind.[9]

This seems a perfectly serviceable definition. The problem for John is
that there is nothing in it that need apply only to the capitalist nation-states
of recent times. It could be applied to any state in any period. Provided we
have an invented 'nation' (or 'people' or 'tribe' or whatever the imagined
cultural entity happens to be), and provided this imagined group is associated with a particular state or prospective state, we have nationalism—ie an
ideology promoting identification between the group and the state that pur-
ports to represent it. Engels, let us recall, argued that the state arose out of
the contradictions inherent in class society: without 'armed bodies of men',
the social order—at root, ruling class control over surplus—could not have
endured.[10] The state, in other words, is an apparatus for the defence of

surplus against both subject populations and rival states. It is therefore an essential feature of *all* class societies.

Nationalism has its root not in any particular form of state, but in the state itself—it is, in essence, a ruling class ideology geared to mobilising support for the state. Hobsbawm is right to argue that the 'nations' of modern nationalism are invented, but John is quite wrong to argue that invented 'nations' are new to history. The process of invention—of nations, peoples, tribes, 'cultural identities'—can be traced backwards through the historical record until we lose sight of it in the grey mist of prehistory. The ancient literature is full of it. The Roman historian Livy frets that his 'passion for Rome's past' might impair his judgement, since he believes 'that no country has ever been greater or purer than ours, or richer in good citizens and noble deeds'.[11] Thucydides has the Greek politician Perikles speak of 'the greatness of Athens' and men 'falling in love with her', as he delivers a funeral oration for the city's war dead.[12] God announces to Moses, the leader of a band of stateless refugees wandering in the desert, that 'if you obey my voice and keep my covenant, you shall be my treasured possession out of all the peoples... You shall be for me a priestly kingdom and a holy nation'.[13] Much of the Hebrew Bible—or Christian 'Old Testament'—can in fact be read as a nationalist tract supporting the state-building aspirations of the ancient Jewish ruling class—and a nationalist tract of the most virulent kind, with its advocacy of imperialist war, ethnic cleansing and wholesale colonisation.[14]

There was, moreover, no Chinese wall between upper class nationalism and lower class reformism. Just as modern nationalists have mobilised peasant populations in 'national liberation struggles' by supporting social reform, so too, we can safely assume, did ancient ones. Josephus—our principal source for the Jewish Revolution of AD 66-73—may not tell us anything about this, but that proves nothing since he tells us very little altogether about the ideology of the rebels. If, though, we turn to the well documented histories of some of the Greek city-states and of the Roman republic, we find that a central feature of these is the periodic emergence of ruling class politicians advocating a popular programme of land reform and debt cancellation as a way of stabilising the state and maintaining its military cohesion.[15] This meshing of state-building and social reform is also reflected in the Bible: the 'Promised Land' was—theoretically, at least—subject to a periodic 'Jubilee' when slaves were freed, debts lifted and lands restored to their original owners.[16] If Vietnamese peasants fighting landlords, government officials and US soldiers in 1960-1975 were waging some sort of 'national liberation struggle', then so too, I would suggest, were Jewish peasants fighting landlords, government officials and Roman soldiers in AD 66-73.

Ancient racism

John rejects my argument that Roman society was both racist in general and anti-Semitic in particular. The idea that racism is peculiar to capitalist society is widespread among Marxists. When Peter Alexander defined racism in *Racism, Resistance and Revolution*, he put it thus:

> Racism can be properly understood only from a Marxist perspective, which treats it as an historically specific, materially caused phenomenon. Racism is not, as is widely assumed, a universal feature of all societies. In the sense of discrimination against a group on the grounds of some imputed inherited characteristic, such as colour, racism is a product of capitalism.[17]

Why a product of capitalism only? It is certainly true that forms of racism vary from one society to another—ie racism is 'an historically specific, materially caused phenomenon'—and also that some societies (classless ones) are without racism. But there are strong theoretical and empirical grounds for believing racism of some sort to be a feature of all *class* societies. What, after all, are racism's material roots? First, the division of the world into states, or rather, since the two elements are effectively inseparable, 'nation-states'. State-building ruling classes not only employ nationalism to bind together 'the people' of their states, but also direct racism against the excluded as a justification for pursuing the goals of the nation-state. The excluded may be present within the state—non-citizens, 'metics' (foreigners), slaves, guest workers, asylum seekers—or they may be the external enemies of the state. The second root of racism lies in the competition within society for material benefits that are in scarce supply— land, subsidies, commercial contracts, jobs, housing, and so on. The ruling class uses racism to divide and confuse popular resistance to its own control of surplus, and it finds it easy to embed it in the actual experience of a competitive struggle for survival among the subordinate classes. On these theoretical grounds, we should expect racism in all class societies. We should anticipate its appearance alongside the family, private property and the state at the dawn of history. What is the evidence?

The arguments against ancient racism on empirical grounds are desperately weak. This comment of John's is typical:

> But slaves, Jewish or otherwise, could obtain manumission, their 'freedom', and become Roman citizens. And very large numbers did so. This could not have been possible in a racist state.[18]

Or there is this from Chris Harman:

> Many important figures in Roman history came from north Africa, including at least one emperor; no text bothers to mention whether they were light or dark skinned.[19]

By the same token, given that Colin Powell, the head of the US armed forces, is black, we would have to conclude that the modern United States is not racist. Chris continues in the same passage:

> There was deep hostility to the Jews in medieval Europe. But this was hostility on the basis of religion...not on the basis of allegedly inherent physical or mental characteristics... What was involved was irrational religious hatred, not irrational biological racism.[20]

I do not believe the distinction Chris is drawing here—between 'irrational religious hatred' and 'irrational biological racism'—has any great significance. If racism is rooted in the competition between states, groups and individuals in class society, and if it is fostered by the ruling class in response to these contradictions, it cannot be defined by something so trivial as an ideological nuance. Nor, in practice, do we do this. 'Biological racism' is not, in fact, the dominant form of racism today; this idea is largely restricted to the fascist right. Much more widespread is one form or another of 'cultural racism'. When told by a leading politician that an 'alien culture' is threatening to 'swamp us', we regard this as racism. When Muslim culture is accused of fostering 'terrorism', we do not describe this as merely an 'irrational religious hatred'. Rightly so. Racists do not make subtle distinctions between religion, nationality and race when choosing their targets. The forms of racism vary, the choice of victim often determined by historical traditions, but we deal with essentially the same phenomenon whether it is Nazis claiming biological supremacy for the 'master race', New Labour politicians persecuting asylum seekers as 'scroungers', or a Hindu chauvinist mob attacking a Muslim mosque.

Racism in antiquity may not have involved pseudo-scientific claims about the biological inferiority of the oppressed. But pseudo-science is, of course, an ideological form peculiar to capitalism. There is no question, however, that ancient literature contains countless statements of cultural racism, and quite a few that consider the assumed differences to be innate. The source evidence has been synthesised in a splendid book called *Romans and Aliens* by the late ancient historian J P V D Balsdon:[21] 'For years now, the Syrian Orontes [a major river] has poured its sewage into our native Tiber—its lingo and manners, its flutes, its outlandish harps...its native tambourines, and the whores who hang out round the circus'.[22] Thus the Latin poet Juvenal. What is one to call this sort of thing if not 'racism'? Or there is this from Cicero: 'Syrians were born slaves, like Jews'.[23] I find it difficult to conceive of a more categorical statement of biological inferiority than this. John quotes this in his review, announcing airily that it is nothing more than 'social class snobbery and the celebration of Roman "civilisation" over and above other, "lesser" beings'.[24] Lesser? In what sense? Well, Cicero tells us, does he not? Born fit for slavery—lesser in that very biological sense. Cicero, moreover, is mainstream and typical—always reliably on-message about Roman aristocratic values. That the Romans had a strong sense of their inherited biological superiority is, in fact, implicit in many texts. In Virgil's *Aeneid*, we are told that the divinely ordained destiny of the Roman 'race'—the Latin word *genus* is explicitly biological—was to rule the world.[25] The Romans, in other words, took it for granted that they were antiquity's 'master race'.

Racism was inherent in the ancient world because, like the modern, it was divided into classes and states. It is therefore no surprise to find it in abundance in the ancient texts.

Was Jesus a revolutionary?

John denounces me for 'recruiting Jesus as one of the leading revolutionary cadres' and for 'enveloping the whole discussion in an aura of religious mysticism'.[26] To describe Jesus thus—which I do not—is too strong.[27] It is, however, possible to interpret him as a messiah in the traditional Jewish sense—which means not the god-man of Christian belief, but a special prophet-king who leads the people of Israel in the apocalyptic battles at the end of time to rid the world of corruption and injustice. Jesus may, that is, have been a revolutionary millenarian of a kind familiar through much of ancient and medieval history. If so, he was a dangerous political subversive, one of several known to us in the sources for 1st century Palestine, and it is hardly surprising that he was arrested and executed by the imperial authorities.

This interpretation is based on a critical reading of the Gospels in the context of other evidence for the period.[28] I claim no credit for either method or conclusion. To repeat, *Apocalypse* is a work of synthesis, not primary scholarship, and the discovery of a revolutionary millenarian Jesus in the Gospels is not new. John does not accept this reading of the texts, but he does not engage directly in the argument, contenting himself with references to alternative scholarship. There is therefore nothing more to be said here, except for me to voice two concerns. I think John is altogether too trusting of the judgements of non-Marxist scholars who (a) do not employ a dialectical method, and (b) do not accept the centrality of the class struggle in history. Mastery of a body of evidence is one thing; the ability to fit material into a wider historical framework is quite another. One common error among specialist scholars is to interpret the past in terms of rigid categories. Jesus has to be something definite: a Pharisee, an Essene, a Zealot, a Gnostic, or, for Geza Vermes in *Jesus the Jew* (which John mentions approvingly), 'one of the holy miracle-workers of Galilee'.[29] But history is not formed of rigid categories. It is a process, a sequence of changes, a dynamic clash of contradictions in which both the people who make history and the history they make are in flux. Jesus does not need a label—he needs a context. How he, his followers and his enemies understood the situation was undoubtedly contested and changeable—as in any living movement.

The second problem is that non-Marxist scholars consistently downplay the possibility of popular self activity unless there are explicit references to this in written sources. Moreover, when confronted by it, they are often willing to take at face value the hostile critiques of ancient commentators. Martin Goodman is a case in point. I do take his work seriously, but as a Marxist I reject his revisionist conclusions, for he follows his source—Josephus—in turning the Jewish Revolution of AD 66-73 into a mere factional struggle for power between self interested politicians.[30] We can do better. Using 'modern analytical concepts'—Marxism—we can read our sources critically, place the class struggle at the centre of events, and so attempt to understand ancient history properly.

NOTES

1: A paperback edition of *Apocalypse: The Great Jewish Revolt Against Rome, AD 66-73* will be available in paperback from Tempus in January 2004, price £12.99.

2: J Rose, 'The Jubilee and the Apocalypse', *International Socialism* 98 (Spring 2003), pp117-118.

3: As above, p117.

4: G E M de Ste Croix, *The Class Struggle in the Ancient Greek World* (Duckworth, 1981), pp3-30.

5: The definition offered in J Molyneux, 'What is the Real Marxist Tradition?', *International Socialism* 20 (Summer 1983), pp3-53.

6: G E M de Ste Croix, as above, p35.

7: J Rose, as above, pp118-119.

8: The two key works are E Hobsbawm and T Ranger (eds), *The Invention of Tradition* (Cambridge University Press, 1983), and E Hobsbawm, *Nations and Nationalism since 1780: Programme, Myth, Reality* (Cambridge University Press, 1990).

9: E Hobsbawm, as above, p9.

10: F Engels, *The Origin of the Family, Private Property and the State* (New York, 1972). Engels' argument is, of course, that all the primary features of class society necessarily arise at the same point in history. I would extend the argument to include nationalism and racism, since these are essentially ideological expressions of a division of the world into states.

11: Livy, *The Early History of Rome* (Penguin, 1960), p18.

12: Thucydides, *The Peloponnesian War* (Penguin, 1972), p149.

13: Exodus 19:5-6.

14: An excellent study of this is R Lane Fox's *The Unauthorized Version: Truth and Fiction in the Bible* (Viking, 1991). See N Faulkner, *Apocalypse: The Great Jewish Revolt Against Rome, AD 66-73* (Tempus, 2002), pp68-73, for a summary.

15: This was especially true of the Greek *turannoi* ('tyrants') and the Roman *populares* ('populists')—in both cases, aristocratic politicians with reformist programmes and popular mass bases.

16: N Faulkner, as above, pp116-117.

17: P Alexander, *Racism, Resistance and Revolution* (Bookmarks, 1987), pp1-2.

18: J Rose, as above, p119.

19: C Harman, *A People's History of the World* (Bookmarks, 1999), p252.

20: As above.

21: J P V D Balsdon, *Romans and Aliens* (Duckworth, 1979).

22: Juvenal, *The Sixteen Satires* (Penguin, 1974), p89.

23: Quoted in J P V D Balsdon, as above, p67.

24: J Rose, as above, pp118-119.

25: There are many such references, but the best known is Virgil, *The Aeneid* (Penguin, 1958), pp172-173.

26: J Rose, as above, pp120-121.

27: John's implication that I portray Jesus as if he were the leader of a group like the Jacobins or the Bolsheviks is unfair. I believe he was a charismatic religious leader who almost certainly inspired millenarian expectations in his followers, but I make no attempt to argue that this makes his movement comparable with modern revolutionary parties. Indeed, the relative incoherence and nebulousness of the Jewish revolutionary movement in AD 66-73 is, I would suggest, one of its key characteristics.

28: N Faulkner, as above, pp97-101.

29: G Vermes, *Jesus the Jew* (SCM Classics, 2001), pp195-197.

30: This is the argument in M Goodman, *The Ruling Class of Judaea: The Origins of the Jewish Revolt Against Rome, AD 66-70* (Cambridge University Press, 1987). The title reflects the perspective accurately.

The Socialist Workers Party is one of an international grouping of socialist organisations:

Australia International Socialist Organisation, PO Box A338, Sydney South. *iso@iso.org.au*

Austria Linkswende, Postfach 87, 1108 Wien. *linkswende@yahoo.com*

Britain Socialist Workers Party, PO Box 82, London E3 3LH. *enquiries@swp.org.uk*

Canada International Socialists, PO Box 339, Station E, Toronto, Ontario M6H 4E3. *iscanada@on.aibn.com*

Cyprus Ergatiki Demokratia, PO Box 27280, Nicosia. *wd@workersdemocracy.net*

Czech Republic Socialisticka Solidarita, PO Box 1002, 11121 Praha 1. *socsol@email.cz*

Denmark Internationale Socialister, PO Box 5113, 8100 Aarhus C. *intsoc@socialister.dk*

Finland Sosialistiliitto, PL 288, 00171 Helsinki. *info@sosialistiliitto.org*

France Socialisme par en bas, BP 15-94111, Arcueil Cedex. *contact@socialismeparenbas.org*

Germany Linksruck, Postfach 44 0346, 12003 Berlin. *info@linksruck.de*

Ghana International Socialist Organisation, PO Box TF202, Trade Fair, Labadi, Accra. *isogh@hotmail.com*

Greece Sosialistiko Ergatiko Komma, c/o Workers Solidarity, PO Box 8161, Athens 100 10. *sek@otenet.gr*

Holland Internationale Socialisten, PO Box 92025, 1090AA Amsterdam. *info@internationalesocialisten.org*

Ireland Socialist Workers Party, PO Box 1648, Dublin 8. *swp@clubi.ie*

Italy Comunismo dal Basso, Leeder, CP Bologna, Succ 5. *dalbasso@hotmail.com*

New Zealand Socialist Workers Organisation, PO Box 13-685, Auckland. *socialist-worker@pl.net*

Norway Internasjonale Socialisterr, Postboks 9226, Grønland, 0134 Oslo. *intsos@intsos.no*

Poland Pracownicza Demokracja, PO Box 12, 01-900 Warszawa 118. *pracdem@go2.pl*

Spain En Lucha, Apartado 563, 08080 Barcelona. *info@enlucha.org*

Uruguay Izquierda Revolucionaria. *ir@adinet.com.uy*

Zimbabwe International Socialist Organisation, PO Box 6758, Harare. *isozim@hotmail.com*

The following issues of **International Socialism** (second series) are available price £3 up to **IS 2:99**, £4 from **IS 2:100** (including postage), from IS Journal, PO Box 82, London E3 3LH.
International Socialism 2:58 and **2:65** are available on cassette from the Royal National Institute for the Blind (Peterborough Library Unit). Phone 01733 370 777.

International Socialism 2:100 Autumn 2003
John Rees: Socialism in the 21st century ★ Salma Yaqoob: Global and local echoes of the anti-war movement: a British Muslim perspective ★ Murray Smith: The broad party, the revolutionary party and the united front: a reply ★ Paul McGarr: Steven Jay Gould in perspective ★ James Meadway: Life after capitalism ★ Judy Cox: Can capitalism go on forever?

International Socialism 2:99 Summer 2003
Chris Harman: Analysing imperialism ★ Anne Alexander: Daring for victory ★ Ian Birchall: Michael Kidron (1930–2003) ★ Guido Picelli: The revolt in Parma ★ Brian Manning: The legacy of Christopher Hill ★ Mike Gonzalez: Crying out for revolution ★ Mark Thomas: Philosophy and the masses

International Socialism 2:98 Spring 2003
Sam Ashman: The anti-capitalist movement and the war ★ John Rees: Cairo calling ★ The Cairo Declaration ★ Colin Sparks: Inside the media ★ Mike Gonzalez: In the eye of the storm ★ Robert Sáenz and Isidoro Cruz Bernal: The driving force behind the 'Argentinazo' ★ Rachel Aldred: Between the no longer and the not yet ★ Dave Renton: When superpowers lose ★ Hassan Mahamdallie: Defying the colour line ★ John Rose: The Jubilee and the Apocalypse ★ Jane Hardy: Toil and trouble: the state of the US economy

International Socialism 2:97 Winter 2002
Alex Callinicos: The grand strategy of the American empire ★ Murray Smith: Where is the SWP going? ★ Nick McKerrell: The united front today ★ John Rees: The broad party, the revolutionary party and the united front ★ Gilbert Achcar: Engels: theorist of war, theorist of revolution ★ Dave Crouch: The inevitability of radicalism ★ Sheila McGregor: Neither Washington nor Moscow

International Socialism 2:96 Autumn 2002
Chris Harman: The workers of the world ★ August Nimtz: Class struggle under 'Empire': in defence of Marx and Engels ★ John Bellamy Foster: Marx's ecology in historical perspective ★ Mike Kidron: Failing growth and rampant costs: two ghosts in the machine of modern capitalism ★ Ian Birchall: Zola for the 21st century ★ Jim Wolfreys: The disposable heroes of hypocrisy

International Socialism 2:95 Summer 2002
Hassan Mahamdallie: Racism: myths and realities ★ Jim Wolfreys: 'The centre cannot hold': fascism, the left and the crisis of French politics ★ Daniel Bensaïd: Leaps! Leaps! Leaps! ★ Slavoj Žižek: A cyberspace Lenin—why not? ★ John Rees: Leninism in the 21st century ★ Anne Alexander: Redrawing the political map ★ Sam Ashman: Islam and imperialism ★ Megan Trudell: From tangentopoli to Genoa

International Socialism 2:94 Spring 2002
Chris Harman: Argentina: rebellion at the sharp end of the world crisis ★ Martin Smith: The return of the rank and file? ★ Leo Zeilig: Crisis in Zimbabwe ★ Jim Wolfreys: Pierre Bourdieu: voice of resistance ★ Richard Greeman: Memoirs of a revolutionary ★ Dave Crouch: The seeds of national liberation

International Socialism 2:93 Special issue
John Rees: Imperialism: globalisation, the state and war ★ Jonathan Neale: The long torment of Afghanistan ★ Anne Alexander: The crisis in the Middle East ★ Mike Gonzalez: The poisoned embrace: Plan Colombia and the expansion of imperial power ★ Chris Harman: The new world recession

Please phone 020 7538 3308 if you require an issue not shown here